Fahfangoolah!

Fahfangoolah!
The despised and indispensable *Welcome to Woop Woop*

Michael Winkler

Copyright © Michael Winkler, 2016
This book is copyright. Apart from any fair dealing for the purpose of private study, research, criticism or review, as permitted under the Copyright Act, no part may be reproduced by any process without written permission.
The moral right of the author has been asserted.

Cover design by Joe Winkler
Line art drawing of cockatoo from archives of Pearson Scott Foresman: Wikimedia Commons.

National Library of Australia CIP Data

Creator: Winkler, Michael, author.

Title: Fahfangoolah! : the despised and indispensable Welcome to Woop Woop / Michael Winkler.

ISBN: 9780994579805 (paperback)

Subjects: Welcome to Woop Woop (Motion picture : 1997)
  Comedy films--Northern Territory--History and criticism.
  Motion picture authorship--Northern Territory.

Dewey Number: 791.43617

Westbourne Books
www.michaelwinkler.com.au

CONTENTS

One film	7
Wild, warped, wonky, weird, wanton, wayward – and worthwhile	9
Rod Taylor and Johnathon Schaech	30
Making it	37
Hearts of Darkness: The Musical	43
Cannes	55
Backlash	59
The look	69
The sound	74
The book	77
Unconnected further thoughts	81
Being Stephan Elliott	88
Fitting *Welcome to Woop Woop* within the Elliott oeuvre	95
Three older cousins of *Welcome to Woop Woop*	106
Welcome to Woop Woop and the outback in Australian cinema	112
Indigenous Australia and the outback film	120
The cannibalism conceit	127
Appendix I: Outback tropefest	131
Appendix II: Ask for it by name	141
Appendix III: Films referred to in this book	142
Notes	149

One film

Imagine this unhappy scenario: all Australian films from the first century of local cinema are to be destroyed – except one. Which would you save?

One film only, to represent a century of Australian cinema.

There are claims for the astonishing *Picnic at Hanging Rock* and the devastating *Wake in Fright*. There might be arguments for the nation-forming narratives of *Breaker Morant*, *Gallipoli* or even *Don's Party*. If populism counts, *Crocodile Dundee* took a Bowie knife to existing box office records, and various *Mad Max* iterations proved that we can make genre films as well here as anywhere.

The Story of the Kelly Gang and *Jedda* have historical significance if not inherent value. Various sentimental favourites will flicker to mind before being easily dismissed: *The Year My Voice Broke*, *Bad Boy Bubby*, *They're a Weird Mob*, *Muriel's Wedding* or one of the *On Our Selection*s might be popular candidates.[1]

But we only get to choose one. And none of that list, taken alone, properly represents the first century of Aussie film.

No, the best choice, like it or not, is *Welcome to Woop Woop*.

With every other 1999-and-before movie wiped, *Welcome to Woop Woop* preserves the elements that differentiated Australian cinema from that of other nations in the twentieth century: a regional stamp that combined cheekiness, energy, wit and a vivid visual sense. It is more interesting than the vast majority of flicks of its era, and encapsulates crucial elements of the national psyche like no other movie. It would be possible to teach a class on Australian film using *Welcome to Woop Woop* as the only text. In addition, it is sociologically significant, both in what the film says about Australia of the recent past, and what the local response to it says about Australia now. It is a prime exemplar of the most prominent genre in the Australian film canon, the outback movie. And, as it happens, it comes with a rollicking making-of story that embodies a strain of larrikin can-do we would all like to claim as dinkum.

However, before we reverently entomb Stephan Elliott's dystopic curio in a lead-lined museum case, preserved for cinephiles of future millennia, some notes are needed for cultural historians yet unborn.

Hence this book.

Wild, warped, wonky, weird, wanton, wayward – and worthwhile

Ever since its release, *Welcome to Woop Woop* has been regarded as the grotesque idiot nephew of the Australian cultural family. A national embarrassment. An opportunity for critics to one-up each other in snark:

"...a dusty, sunburnt outback romp very like *Priscilla*, apart from the fact it has five per cent of the laughs and none of the dress sense." (Jim Schembri, The Age)

"...a movie that stinks slightly higher than a dead kangaroo on the side of the road..." (Clark Forbes, Sunday Herald Sun)

"...a meandering goof in search of a purpose..." (Jack Mathews, Los Angeles Times)

"...the culinary equivalent of loading a mad, rotting, random selection of ingredients into a pot, hoping for the best, and getting indigestible, garbage-disposal fodder." (Annette Basile, FilmInk[2])

"Many Australian films are about retards. This was directed by one...a no effort, useless, pointless, moronic piece of excrement." (Chris Parry, EFilmCritic)

"...a brutal chore to sit through. The violence is too foul to be funny, and the 'jokes' are mostly just stupid...I made sure to take a hot shower when I got home."
(Paul Tatara, CNN)

If Australian cinema is Cooper Pedy, then *Welcome to Woop Woop* is a unique uncut opal which has been chucked away behind the mining camp dunny. It deserves better.

The film premiered in Sydney on 12 August 1998. It was the third feature for Stephan Elliott, after *Frauds* and *The Adventures of Priscilla, Queen of the Desert*. Its three stars were veteran Australian Rod Taylor, a long-term expatriate; Susie Porter, an emerging talent from Newcastle; and handsome American leading man Johnathon Schaech. It was based on a novel by Douglas Kennedy, 'The Dead Heart'. The screenplay was written by Michael Thomas with input from Elliott. It was backed by Goldwyn Entertainment Company, the Australian Film Finance Corporation and Scala Productions in association with Unthank Films. It was a twist on the familiar fish-out-of-water scenario, a standard three-act plot occurring within the well-worn setting of an isolated community that adheres to its own set of rules.

But it was, and is, much more than that.

"No-one got it," said legendary costume designer Lizzy Gardiner. "It was the retarded thirty-year-old child that only a mother could love. I think it's possibly the best film I was ever involved with. I love every moment of it."

"We aspired to boffo," reflected screenplay writer Thomas. "Instead it's a cult."

Almost two decades after its release, the movie continues to find friends – people who happen across it and can meet it on its own terms, unphased by the rancorous original reviews. "It's just grown and grown and grown," Elliott said. "It's mostly filmmakers that have come out of the woodwork saying that they love it. But when I eventually met RuPaul, he/she said, '*Priscilla* is a pile of shit. *Welcome To Woop Woop* is the greatest movie ever made!' When there was a competition to name the ten greatest Australian films ever made, which they were going to put on postage stamps, they put twenty films up for people to vote for the best ten. *Priscilla* came second, and *The Castle* came first, which I still scratch my head about. I still don't get it. But anyway, there was this massive online wave of people asking why *Welcome To Woop Woop* wasn't on the list. That was about ten years ago, and that's when I realised that there were bootleg copies of the film floating around. This cult has grown around it.

"The amount of people coming out of the woodwork who have discovered it and get the joke many years down the line even in its unbalanced, unfinished form is amazing. I had Tom Ford walk up to me at the Oscars and say that it's one of his favourite films."[3] Fashion legend Ford has held *Woop Woop*-themed parties, and reportedly made a rip-off version of Duffy's stars-and-stripes suit for himself.

Writer Michael Brissenden recalled with some astonishment meeting a homeless Vietnam vet in Las Vegas who, when he heard he was Australian, asked Brissenden the location of Woop Woop. The veteran's interest was piqued by having once seen the movie that "Had this really horny chick in it". He also wanted to know "Is it true that you all kill kangaroos for dog food?"[4]

Susie Porter reported her surprise at sitting next to director Robert Luketic (*Legally Blonde*) on a judging panel and having him quote *Welcome to Woop Woop* lines at her from heart, including, 'You're just a dry sandwich. You couldn't get a root in a frankfurt factory.'

The wonder is that the movie was made at all. The shoot was horrendously hard. The financiers in LA were horrified by the rushes they saw beamed through from the Australian desert. The director's health was precarious. The international lead was tormented by flies, heat, self-doubt and limited comedic potential. The veteran star holding the film together had a body that was falling apart. The young female lead, a passionate animal rights activist, was placed in a truck full of slaughtered kangaroos, surrounded by dead dogs. And all the time the story emerging on celluloid moved further and further away from the one the producers thought was being told. All of this was before humiliation at the world's biggest film festival, butchery in the edit suite, and the gleeful malignancy of Australian critics who did not just cut down tall poppy Elliott but gleefully put his movie through the mulcher.

Elliott calls it a "spectacular car crash". The Australian film industry has not had enough of them. *Welcome to Woop Woop* pushed way beyond the prevailing ethos of the quirky-cute Aussie indie film – a deceptively safe envelope of middle-brow moderation dressed up to look vaguely daring – and would have gone further if the director had been given his head. The final cut was badly compromised, but there is enough that is radical and meaningful in the finished film to give it continued contemporary relevance, and provide pleasures beyond mere shock value.

The movie was a ghastly box-office failure but it is something autochthonous, something that could only be torn from the middle of this strange and wonderful country, and that singularity is increasingly rare. Rather than conforming to a cuddly mass-sanctioned idea of Australia, *Welcome to Woop Woop* unapologetically strip-mines one iteration of the nation, and appeases no-one. The Australia it anatomises and traduces is going, almost gone, but to deny it ever existed (and still exists in pockets) means erasing part of our national foundation. It is simultaneously an act of celebrating, critiquing and determinedly not-forgetting. Elliott's 'failure' to spell out exactly how we should feel about the small but significant subset of Australians represented in his film indicates that he is an artist, not a sloganeer, but that fundamental distinction did not save him from a critical puzzling.

Another reason this strange and deeply flawed movie matters is because of its unique position within the pantheon of Australian films. The syllogism goes like this: Historically and culturally, the outback film is the quintessential Australian film. *Welcome to Woop Woop* incorporates more elements of the outback film than any other movie. Therefore *Welcome to Woop Woop* is the quintessential Australian film.

Perhaps that bow is drawn too long, and of course nothing will convince some people that the movie has even a skerrick of worth. Regardless, the story of how the film was made, and how it (and its director) fell Icarus-like to earth is instructive. It is also a reminder that, despite the omnipotence of financial dictates, there is still a lunatic dynamism in movie-making that sets it apart from every other industry.

This is the story: Teddy (Schaech) is a New York hustler who escapes to Australia when a rare bird scam goes violently wrong. In the deep outback he meets and falls for sexually aggressive Angie (Porter), who tricks him into marriage and drags him back to her home town, Woop Woop. It is officially 'off the map', a forgotten place ruled by the despotic Daddy-O (Taylor) who decrees that no-one leaves town without his permission – and permission is never given. Teddy is increasingly alarmed by the craziness of Woop Woop and seeks the help of schoolteacher Krystal (Dee Smart) as he tries to escape.

Plotwise, that's about it – but plot is rarely paramount in films of lasting interest. The natural landscape and the built environment compete with an off-the-leash Taylor for top billing, followed closely by the remarkable song list, extraordinary dialogue, accomplished cinematography, the nitro-glycerine instability of Porter's Angie, plus the costuming, set design and attention to every last visual detail.

The dialogue is simultaneously singular and deeply familiar. "The point is, you poked me, mate. You did me like a dinner." "Personally I can't see what she sees in a hippy-looking numbat like you." The new bride saying, "Now where are those fuckin' wedding photos?"

"Happy as a bastard on Father's Day." And the delicate discussion on manual methods which must be employed so as to avoid inappropriate inter-familial sexual activity: "You beat your meat. You flog your log. You wank your shank. You pull your pud."

There is a similar glorying in kitsch Australiana. Maxwell House coffee. Flip-up sunglasses. Lemon meringue. Kewpie dolls. The seven o'clock news. Buffalo horns. Communal cricket games. The preponderance of tinned pineapple in savoury dishes which reached epidemic proportions at one low point in the nation's culinary history. Spectacles mended with sticky-tape. The Hill's Hoist.

Critics who understood what Elliott was aiming for when the film was first released are still advocates today. Louise Keller of Urban Cinefile said, "At the time there were a few turned up noses at my [positive] review – but that has never worried me. My opinion of the film has not changed. When I first saw it before release, I found it quite pure in its absurdity and wickedly bold in that it was unafraid to be outrageous, rude and crude. It is very Steph Elliott and I like and admire his work enormously. He has the capacity for such range but his sense of humour is uniquely Steph."

Adrian Martin, now an Associate Professor in the Arts Faculty at Monash University, wrote a broadminded review for The Age. "My opinion of this strange and amazing film remains exactly the same," he said in 2016. "I watched some of it again on TV recently, and was confirmed in my estimation of it back in 1998 – which was pretty positive, as distinct from most of my reviewer colleagues of the era. These days, it's a film I recommend heartily to film lovers (and connoisseurs of the bizarre) in countries beyond Australia. It's also, in retrospect, the last interesting film (in my opinion) by Elliott, in fact his finest hour. He wasn't entirely in control of everything his film was doing and saying, but this chaos-factor worked well for him here (for once)."

Tara Judah argued that the film has been "easily dismissed" because its purported crassness was not mitigated by being endearing. "It's dark and admittedly daft, but somewhere beneath its damaging depiction of the detritus of contemporary Australian culture lies a harsh historicality; an indubitable landscape, unpleasant and unforgiving... Perhaps, in retrospect, it is easier to consider the merits of the film as we find ourselves now situated in an era of post-reconciliation? Or perhaps audiences will never be ready for Woop Woop – its unforgiving landscape a mark of its audacity to dare broach the question of Australian identity without apology and devoid of empathy?"[5] Deb Verhoeven was another influential voice who argued that it was not the 'abomination'[6] of popular memory.

The film was given the backhanded honour of inclusion in the Foxtel World Movies channel Cult: Best of the Worst mini-festival in 2015. "I am particularly excited to present *Welcome to Woop Woop*, one of my all-time Aussie classics, which I think is way overdue for a new re-evaluation," said host Andrew Mercado. In fact, Mercado has been a fan of the film since first release. "There was so much negativity about the film. It was universally panned on its release and only found its cult audience afterwards and that is how many so-called bad films live on when others are forgotten. It is no surprise to me that *Woop Woop* is now a cult classic because it's got everything such movies need – top notch casting, quotable dialogue, memorable music, crazy costumes, black humour and those batshit crazy cameos which begin with Ginger Grant from Gilligan's Island and end with two now-forgotten 'dole bludgers' after the credits.

"The saddest thing about *Woop Woop*'s failure is that Rod Taylor didn't get recognised for his towering performance as Daddy-O. He reminded me of many, many old blokes I grew up with and still knew and that's why I was always mystified that so many critics thought the movie was dated. I have watched *Woop Woop* multiple times over the years but after one long absence of not watching it, Rod Taylor really unnerved me. Maybe because I thought the film was so funny on the first viewings, I had missed how terrifying he actually was.

"Several years after its release, I interviewed Susie Porter about some other serious and therefore more important Australian movie – but as soon as the cameras were switched off, I started raving about *Woop Woop*. She assured me that I was far from the first fan who wanted to know more. That's when I realised that it had finally become a fully-fledged cult hit," Mercado said.

When critic Luke Buckmaster rewatched the movie for The Guardian in 2015 he found, "a gloriously batty and bittersweet love letter to the idea of Australian identity... Like the broken relics and weird thingamebobs strewn across the set, Elliott's second (sic) film is kitschy and anachronistic, and doesn't feel like it belongs to a particular time. Perhaps it will just keep getting better."[7]

A more accurate summation may have been: perhaps the world will keep catching up to Elliott's vision, his "glib, hyperactive frivolity" [8] to use producer Al Clark's phrase, his affectionate ruthlessness towards his characters and his country.

Our way in to the story appears to be through Teddy, but after a while we discard him. He's too American. He's not us. Teddy is poised, Blaise Pascal-style, between the infinite and the abyss. There is nothing he can reasonably expect in Woop Woop apart from time. Time that stretches into forever, like the outback landscape itself. The way he dissolves into the interior tugs at a great fear embedded in the collective Australian unconscious. The outback is big enough to absorb any individual without trace, but when it is a lone international visitor there will not even be a search party. "The narrative of disappearance is a strong thread in Australian history – convicts, explorers, shipwreck survivors, gold-seekers, adult settlers as well as children – all are recorded as having disappeared," wrote Kim Torney. "Even those who disappeared from the land rather than into it, such as the young soldiers who sailed away to die overseas, have reinforced this sense that disappearance is an innate part of the national experience."[9] For Teddy, it becomes the centre of his international experience.

The American made one misjudgement, saying yes too vigorously to Angie, a young woman both eff-able and ineffable. Hardly an error deserving the punishment of a life sentence. However, that is the way drama works. One poor decision, or one moment of moral weakness, leads to a grand unravelling. It is the mainspring of movies as varied as Scorsese's *After Hours* and the Steve Carell-Tina Fey vehicle *Date Night*, as well as Shakespearean tragedies and children's stories from most cultures and most times.

Because Teddy is not wholly sympathetic, we are invited to take Krystal as our central point of identification. It is easy to imagine being part of a family but not feeling a sense of belonging. We understand the burden Krystal carries of simultaneously seeing through what is going on, while remaining part of it. She has to balance loyalty to her family and the community against the realisation that life in Woop Woop is unhealthy and its citizens are unhinged. (Smart's Krystal is the film's least successful character. She sways between sassy and shy, between staying in lock-step with local ways and thinking independently. If Krystal is indeed the "unopened dry sandwich" that Angie claims she is, it is unlikely that she would show so much confidence in her flirtation with Teddy. And if she is sufficiently horrified by the town's barbarism that she wants to escape, it is odd that she seems so little moved by the execution of her husband Midget – even though she knows his summary punishment is in line with town rules.)

By contrast, Taylor's Daddy-O is a superb creation who approaches the stature of a biblical figure, a snorting secular Moses. When the CMG asbestos mine exploded (leaving the nearby town of Woop Woop isolated and purposeless) it burned for forty days, reminiscent of both Jesus' forty days in the wilderness and Moses' forty years leading his tribe in the desert. Daddy-O is potent and unchallengeable, a self-appointed leader who maintains discipline with his fists. He is the keeper of the local Commandments, so when the code of the tribe is breached – such as when Duffy and Laverne have sex – he provides rough, public justice. "Duffy you stinking little fucking moll," he says before punching the younger man stupid while forcing him to recite the rules of the community.

Daddy-O is supported by Moose, a leering and laconic figure, Chad Morgan with better dentistry, who represents the lumpen follower. Richard Moir is Reggie, the brightest of the bunch, keeper of the Woop Woop pharmacy, well-spoken DJ and the man who tries to provide a bridge to the town's mores for Teddy. He is the individual who should know better but chooses to support the leader rather than challenging his wrongdoing, either because it is the easy path or because he is in thrall to the strongman, or both. His type is invaluable to any dictatorial regime.

These characters are caricatured, certainly, but not ciphers. Consequently there are moments of genuine emotion amidst the mayhem: Angie's face when she first realises that Teddy fancies her; the tenderness Daddy-O shows towards Ginger as he carries her to the top of the garbage pyre; Krystal's pride when she assists Teddy with his magic trick. This is important, because without these glimpses of humanity, the film's satire would seem not just harsh but pointless. Instead, a world is constructed that we can enter emotionally rather than merely observing with uninvolved detachment.

Susan Dermody and Elizabeth Jacka identified a Gothic tradition in Australian cinema, exemplified by characters that are forged from "deliberately pathological, rather than social or psychological" stereotypes.[10] The grotesques of Woop Woop are not impossibly far removed from reality. Exaggerated, caricatured, made extreme – yes. But they are recognisable, both within rural Australia as we know it, and within Australian film. Tom O'Regan wrote of, "Australian cinema's penchant for producing 'freaks' (like Mick Dundee, Barry McKenzie, Sweetie and Muriel) and 'monsters' (*Razorback*, the men in *Wake in Fright* and *Don's Party*)"[11] and both breeds can be found in Elliott's film. O'Regan noted that, "Many Australian stories focus on people who would be in the periphery, and cast physical types into central roles who would normally be cast into supporting roles…this centring of the ordinary, the daggy (unstylish), the ugly and the mundane."[12] This is one of the glories of the local industry – dagginess and mundanity are elevated, even venerated – and it reaches an apotheosis in *Welcome to Woop Woop*.[13]

Indeed, Woopites might be those scorned in 'The Communist Manifesto' as "social scum, that passively rotting mass thrown off by the lowest layers of old society (which) may, here and there, be swept into the movement by a proletarian revolution; its conditions of life, however, prepare it far more for the part of a bribed tool of reactionary intrigue."[14]

Karl and Friedrich could be describing Woop Woop's founding fathers. Their (possibly justifiable) antipathy to Canberra explains why the people of Woop Woop are where they are, but it does not exonerate the regular citizens from their frantic willingness to fall into lock-step with the reactionary dictates of the town's big men. Which is all very well and easy to say. But who among us would stand up to Daddy-O?

Opposing the overlord means being forced to the outer. Asked whether being gay has influenced his work at all, Elliott said, "there is definitely a feeling through every film and in everything I've ever written that has only recently dawned on me – and that is that I've always felt like a bit of an outsider. Every film I've done is about an outsider not fitting in."[15] The trick with *Welcome to Woop Woop* is to pick the outsider. Superficially it is Teddy, but he represents the most powerful culture on earth. The true outsider is the entire desert community, shunned by a nation that does not know or care that it exists.

While there appears to be a revisionist spirit abroad amongst many of those reconsidering the film, hindsight has not eased the horror for other Australian critics. Andrew McGregor, writing in 2010, claimed the film, "sets its sights on a celebration of Australian 'ockerism' and the works of Rogers (sic) and Hammerstein, with the narrative evidently coming a distant third...regarded by critics in Australia as a national embarrassment, pandering to the most crass of cultural stereotypes."[16]

Journalist Michael Bodey charged that it was, "hubris that allowed him (Elliott) to make the coarse, boisterous comedy *Welcome to Woop Woop* after *Priscilla*."[17] 'Hubris', of course, being a fancy word for getting a bit too big for your boots, the great Australian no-no.

For a film that hardly anyone paid to see on first release, *Welcome to Woop Woop* remains raw in the public consciousness. As recently as October 2015 it was referenced in a debate in the NSW Legislative Council, with The Hon. Dr Peter Phelps pronouncing it "execrable". This was hardly a novel critique. However, Dr Phelps (not to be confused with the Australian actor of the same name) made wider remarks which bear consideration, because they go to the heart of the hatred for the film – and crystallise the widespread but misguided notion that Elliott's previous film succeeded where *Welcome to Woop Woop* failed.

"When one thinks of the Australian bush movies of the 1940s and 1950s one thinks of *The Sundowners*, *Smiley* or something like that—something that played into the general Australian bush mythology of the welcoming country town, mutual support, rugged individualism, industry and productivity," Dr Phelps said. "In many ways that replicated the Hollywood view of the American rural lifestyle as well.

"However—I will not mince words about this—the arts industry in Australia has become overwhelmingly white, urban, bourgeois, progressive and elitist. In many instances it finds working class culture at best problematic and at worst it displays the active disdain of the cosmopolitans for ordinary Australians...But in many instances it is worse than that. From the late 1960s or the early 1970s, from *Wake in Fright* to *Shame* or the execrable *Welcome to Woop Woop* paint a picture of life in rural and regional communities as parochial, narrow-minded, brutal, sexist, racist and homophobic. The people who produced these films congratulate themselves on their moral superiority. They say, 'We are not like these people.' They are missionaries saving the benighted. Indeed, Priscilla is interesting because it breaks from the usual dichotomy of Australian films about the outback. Normally one is given only two choices: leave or die. But Priscilla presents a reconciliation...We should be wary of those who wish to turn rural and regional people into 'the other'. It is easy to demonise what we do not understand one way or the other."[18]

There has always been a strain of nationalism that lionises small towns and posits that bush people are the salt of the earth. This desire to elevate rural dwellers above their city cousins and claim for them some greater moral virtue is far from new – it was the nub of the split more than a century ago between those who favoured 'Banjo' Paterson's portrayal of the bush over that of Barbara Baynton or Henry Lawson. It is a strange but stubborn fantasy that the 'real' Australia is located exactly where most Australians do not live. This is, after all, a highly urbanised country, where more people own stock portfolios than stock whips, and most 4WD vehicles never leave the asphalt. And yet the vast red interior is not only part of our national race memory, but also dominates our cultural iconography. It is fascinating that a nation with such extreme demographic distribution – clinging to the coastal rim like frosting on a glass – maintains a cultural obsession with the desert.[19]

Counteracting the boosterism towards the bush and bushies is an equally persistent, equally unbalanced streak of contempt for what Marx and Engels called "the idiocy of rural life."[20] Small towns can mean small horizons.[21] Justin Heazlewood, who grew up in rural Tasmania, said, "There's a part of me that appreciates my grassroots, no bullshit beginnings, but let's not get carried away. The majority of me despises the narrow minded, 'we hate outsiders, boys don't cry, Jagerbomb, root, have a kid' drought of self-respect."[22] Lou Reed and John Cale sang, "there is only one good use for a small town: you hate it and you'll know you have to leave"[23]. Warren Zevon's take was more rudimentary: "There ain't much to country living: sweat, piss, jizz and blood."[24]

If they can say it, why couldn't Stephan Elliott? Australians habitually struggle with the idea that someone who points out our national flaws might care about the joint as deeply as the loudest members of the mindless Aussie Aussie Aussie Oi Oi Oi brigade. Elliott is not a polemicist; his approach to Woop Woop is simultaneously savage and affectionate. This confused many who saw it.

On the one hand he called it "a love letter" to a disappearing Australia. On the other hand, there was a clear intention to portray the outback quite differently to what he calls the "fluffy" presentation in his previous film. "When I was out there in the desert for *Priscilla*, I saw a side of Australia that I didn't know existed, and it wasn't pretty," he said. "I made the nice sparkly version in *Priscilla*, with one nasty little scene. I saw another side of Australia out there. I nearly got my head bashed in about four times. I thought, 'Okay, hang on, we don't put these parts in *Priscilla*, do we?'"[25]

The 2001 film *Mullet* rings largely false, but it starts with a piece of voiceover which accurately encapsulates the presentation of bush communities in Australian films: "People think that country towns are full of rednecks and gossip, or they think they're about homespun wisdom and preserved fruit." Country towns are presented as delightfully warm-hearted social microcosms, such as in TV series *The Flying Doctors* or *A Country Practice*. In the opposite direction, the representation of small-town bigotry and domestic violence in the ethically dubious[26] *Australian Rules* is so simplistic it takes us further away from truth, not closer to it.

Hick movies have long been a profitable staple of the local industry, starting with Beaumont Smith's 1917 *Our Friends, the Hayseeds*, the first of seven Hayseeds movies. That was followed in close succession by *The Laugh on Dad* (1918) about "an ostrich-farmer who delights in crude practical jokes"; *The Waybacks* (1918), *On Our Selection* (1920) and other movies about the Rudd family; and *Possum Paddock* (1921). It is notable that, when publicising *On Our Selection* in 1920, director Raymond Longford, "criticized the 'ridicule' to which the play had subjected the bush pioneers, which left audiences with the impression 'that our backblocks are populated with a race of unsophisticated idiots'; the sense of humour with which bush people had faced hardships 'has too often been converted into clumsy clowning of the "slapstick" variety' (*Picture Show*, 1 April 1920)."[27]

In 1938 there was another Rudd family chapter with *Dad and Dave Come to Town*. It did not aspire to Longford's ideas about rural nobility. William D. Routt wrote that, "The popularity of (Bert) Bailey and (Edmund) Duggan's *On Our Selection* created a new, specifically Australian, subgenre of rural comedy. The Australian theatrical historian, Margaret Williams, calls this subgenre 'bush comedy'. It is sometimes known as 'backblocks farce' and was called 'farce-bucolical' by at least one critic at the time. This subgenre upended the conventional format of leavening melodrama with occasional flashes of comedy and instead used melodrama – and its narrative line – as an occasional intrusion into a plotless series of broadly comic skits of rural life, exploiting Australian rural dialect, vulgar folk humour and moronic (but nobly stubborn) characterisations of the rural poor."[28]

The outback is no more replete with selfless heroes than the working class is full of people with big hearts and open minds.[29] Prejudice can be found in every social stratum, and country towns can be astonishingly insular. British director David Mallet remembered filming the magical video for David Bowie's 'Let's Dance' at the Carinda Hotel outside Walgett in outback New South Wales. "The scene in the bar was genuine local people who were in the bar at ten in the morning and they hated David Bowie and they hated us – horrible nancy boys making films – so much. Although in the film it looks like they are bopping away and enjoying it they were completely taking the piss out of us. They hated us."[30]

One of the best representations of an outback town is provided by the uncomfortably subcutaneous documentary *Cunnamulla*. Dennis O'Rourke's portrait of the eponymous town is morally questionable; the very thing that makes it so valuable – the closeness he establishes to the locals, and their resultant candour – raises questions of fully-informed consent. Certainly, the heartbreaking 13-year-old Cara and 15-year-old Kelly-Ann who are trying to negotiate the sexual mores of the town, and the dog-catcher and mortician's assistant Herb who lives at the tip, are as memorable as any characters in fictional outback cinema.

This is the tradition within which Elliott was working when he populated the strange world of Woop Woop. He was not afraid to depict rural idiocy, but he did not despise the characters he created. He revelled in their strangeness, and guffawed with them at their own foibles. He gave them Rodgers & Hammerstein, for goodness sake; he allowed them to glory with him in the simple joy of belting out a solid show tune, and in the fun of coming together for shared rituals – however bizarre.

There was scope for Elliott to go even further than he does in *Welcome to Woop Woop*. Or, more correctly, than he does in this, the only cut we have. A comparison can be drawn to Ivan Sen's *Toomelah*, a film made without recourse to the brake pedal. The triumph of *Toomelah* is Sen's determination to sanitise nothing and show everything in his portrait of a remote community gone to hell. There is a peculiar internal logic that has accreted in the community Sen portrays which looks like utter madness from the outside. A place where a little boy is taught to cut up and bag marijuana, where kids and adults call each other 'cunts' without a second thought, where jail time is treated like an exciting holiday away – this is a place of utter madness. It also, horribly, tallies with the truth of some Indigenous communities. While the climactic violence does not quite work, Sen is beholden only to the conventions of the story arc, not to the audience's sensibilities.

(By contrast, Catriona McKenzie's more popular *Satellite Boy* pulls its punches. Both directors, Sen and McKenzie, are Indigenous, but the latter film replaces horror with sadness, hopelessness with hope, and is consequently a more pleasant but less valuable piece of work. Sen's film was shown at a handful of festivals; McKenzie's film, released one year later, was shown on Qantas flights.)

Elliott says that he wants to return to his film and recut it to realise something closer to his original vision. "I'm going back to it, but MGM have been in turmoil, so every time that I've attempted to get in there, I can't, because they're bankrupt," he said. "The thing about *Welcome to Woop Woop* is that I'm not afraid of going back there. I'm not finished with it, and it never got completed. The reaction that it got was absolutely right. But it's funny what an underground cult it's becoming now. I've gotta get in there and take it back. My finished version is even more in your face. It's about bigotry, homophobia, and backwards thinking. Trust me…it's 100 times worse!"[31]

(One example of a scene Elliott would consider reinstating: an "incredibly graphic" sequence of Midget going through the meat grinder and being converted into dog food after he was shot by Daddy-O. The thought of Elliott directing without the brake pedal of financiers and producers is simultaneously exhilarating and terrifying.)

Writing in 1988, Adrian Martin claimed that, "Australian cinema has too often been, since its mid-1970s renaissance, the home of good intentions, liberal ideology and comfortable worthiness."[32] Box-office economics explains this, up to a point; there are films that Aussies will pay to watch, and others that they won't, and some believe that the marketplace is a perfect arbiter. More specifically however, there are some riffs on national identity that turn a buck, and some that flatline on release. One example of the former was Jackie McKimmie's *Australian Dream*, an over-the-top melange of satirical stereotypes, tawdry jokes and vivid interiors, a rejection of the middle-brow in favour of the gloriously gratuitously lowbrow, a powerful skewering of contemporary suburbia – but critics smashed it, and it was hardly shown.

The obverse is *The Castle*, a modest film released sixteen months before *Welcome to Woop Woop* reached Australian screens. The movie is ostensibly about a family of Australian battlers that takes on the combined might of private enterprise and government, and wins. It is really about the stupidity of lower-middle class Australians and their great good fortune that the rich and powerful might, from time to time, give them an even break. Despite this, it was a huge hit.

The movie pretends that its portrayal of the Kerrigan family is gently mocking and affectionate. Its real stance sits somewhere between sneering and sniggering. It is a portrait of a family with some finance but little social capital, constructed by filmmakers who have no idea who these people are, how they live, what they want and how they think. An aggregation of clichés and catchphrases is supposed to plug the hole where characterisation should have been. It is as if, protected from the unwashed unlovelys of Melbourne's northern suburbs while cloistered in expensive private schools and attending the nation's toffiest university, the Working Dog team (which made the film) caught glimpses of the underclass from afar. Then, like archaeologists, they tried to guess how these distant beings lived and thought based on the superficial clues they had collected.

The Kerrigan family is going to be kicked out of its home. Likewise their stereotyped neighbours: a battered woman, an Arab who jokes about terrorism, and a hopeless pensioner. The risible deus ex machina involves a QC taking on their case and winning in the High Court. The battlers are saved by the noblesse oblige of a beneficent toff. The message is: don't worry, little people – those of us on the inside will look after you if we choose to.

The film is narrated by a simpleton with an unexplained level of social and presumably mental retardation. The dopey protagonist, Darryl Kerrigan, is too stupid to be able to distinguish between a law degree and a trade certificate, but has sufficient nous to run his own tow-truck business. His family also owns two houses, multiple cars and a boat, but they are portrayed as poor urban hillbillies. There is a snide reference to Darryl's daughter Tracey completing a hairdressing course at Sunshine TAFE (repeated twice, in case we didn't cringe sufficiently first time around). Sunshine is a low socio-economic suburb on Melbourne's outskirts; it has as much intrinsic worth as anywhere else, but for the Working Dog team its only value is as a punchline.[33]

And yet the film hauled in more than a dozen times its budget in Australia alone, and US rights were sold to Harvey Weinstein's Miramax for a reported $6 million. More than this, it has secured a place as one of the best-loved films produced in this country. Naysayers were and are few. As Felicity Collins and Therese Davis observed,

"The question was asked in the wake of the success of *The Castle*: who was enjoying the film? Seemingly almost everybody. So the conclusion had to be that it was not in poor taste to enjoy it – although it appeared to pour scorn over working-class simpletons and their crummy lives."[34]

What does this say about Australians and how we view ourselves? When *The Castle* is taken into the national bosom but *Welcome to Woop Woop* is demonised it suggests not just a failure of the mass audience's critical faculties, but also the narrow way in which we want to see ourselves represented on screen. Moreover, it suggests that this country of rugged individualists actually craves the fluffy security of a paternalistic system where we rely on the overlords to take care of us. The contrast between the reception for *The Castle* and the reception for *Welcome to Woop Woop* is stark, yet it was the latter film which depicted the characters as agents of their own destiny rather than empty-headed flotsam reliant on being looked after. You want to get Aussies to notice when they are being patronised and looked down on by filmmakers? Tell 'em they're dreaming.

Many people who enjoyed *The Castle* lapped up another successful local film fourteen years later. *Red Dog* did big box-office. It provided a vision of outback Australia that appealed to those citizens who routinely nod along with the talkback radio bleat that, 'We are being made to feel ashamed of who we are as a nation'. The film was set in 1971 and played on nostalgia for a time when men wore singlets and stubbies, when you could tell dumb wogs to shut up, when a bloke could fight another bloke just for the hell of it, and when we didn't have to worry about Abos or feminists or the fact that multinational mining companies are ripping the shit out of the country to make a tiny number of people extremely rich. Sure, *Red Dog* was partly financed by mining giants Rio Tinto and Woodside, but where was the harm in that? Director Kriv Stenders said, "We were incredibly supported by them, it was overwhelming – they were welcoming and excited.

The mining industry has been misaligned [maligned?] recently; it was a chance for them to remind Australians that this is a part of Australia, an amazing, vital part. We were really paying tribute and honour to the pioneers who built the place."[35]

Stenders had previously made the flawed but fascinating *Boxing Day*; it was barely explicable that this was the same director at work. Where *Boxing Day* strove for authenticity, *Red Dog* was a gussied-up nonsense, hiding the truth about men, mining, Australia and the past. Stenders showed outback workers wearing spotless clothes and a 1970s outback pub where there is no cigarette smoke; that mendacious sanitising symbolised the film's whole approach. Local audiences did not seem to notice or care that the American lead (Josh Lucas) is the only character that sees things through the lens of morality. Heck, outback blokes can't be expected to think for themselves, and anyway, isn't that doggy adorable! The lesson, it seems, is that you can never have too much rosy tint when painting Australia for Australian audiences. Escapism is fine, but we should ponder what it is we are actually escaping from.

Meanwhile, we still have *Welcome to Woop Woop*. There were countless 'better' Australian films made in the twentieth century, but none as essential as Elliott's oddity. It is large enough to encompass small town culture and geographic boundlessness, old ockerdom and modern irony, most of the outback film genre's durable tropes, and a sensibility identifiable as Australian from a four-beer drive away. Will cinema studies students of future centuries understand it? Maybe. Probably not. But they might have a bit of fun along the way.

"God bless independent filmmakers who take risks, because in a business that sells product we sometimes make art," Johnathon Schaech said. "Not the other way around."

Rod Taylor and Johnathon Schaech

The great roaring engine that propels *Welcome to Woop Woop* is Daddy-O. With his rare-roast beef face, stentorian bellow and the menace of a cornered taipan, he dominates every square inch of screen. Even when he is not in a scene, the knowledge that he is lurking somewhere is enough to provoke unease. Elliott said, "Rod Taylor *is* the film." Production designer Owen Paterson indicated Taylor's centrality to the entire project when he said, "I tried to create the pub knowing Rod Taylor was going to play Daddy-O. I pictured his face and had a photograph of him, and had a sense that the pub needed to feel well established, almost coming out of the ground."

Taylor was born in Lidcombe in 1930, attended Parramatta High School and started acting in his early twenties. Part of his prize for winning the 1954 Rola Show Australian Radio Actor of the Year Award was a ticket to London. He travelled as far as Los Angeles and stopped. Taylor established a successful career in Stateside television and film, highlighted by lead roles in *The Time Machine* and Alfred Hitchcock's *The Birds*, and billing between Maggie Smith and Orson Welles in the ensemble drama *The V.I.P.s*.

He did not work in Australia for more than two decades. In 1977 he played, ironically, an American in sweet Aussie flick *The Picture Show Man*. Lightly-regarded 1983 drama *On the Run* was the only time he had played an Australian on film prior to *Welcome to Woop Woop*. It is claimed[36] that the role of the rival film distributor in

The Picture Show Man was made into an American to accommodate Taylor's US accent, but as Daddy-O his accent is not just broad Australian but, wonderfully, broad 1950s Australian. The voice is right, the face is fantastic, and he even contributed his own catchphrase: 'Fahfangoolah!'

Taylor was 66, far from Californian backyard pools and air-conditioned studios, stuck in the middle of the red continent ranting like a foul-mouthed psychotic, and he was perfect. Interviewed on set, he said, "It's waiting to burst, the Aussie in me you know. And this [script] seemed to be like a gift: I really fell off the chair laughing and I said: 'I'm damn well doing it, and I'll have a ball here'. And I love Daddy-O; even though he's tyrannosaurus Rex, a dinosaur, he really believes in Australia."[37]

In a different interview he said, "It was the most outrageous comedy I had ever read and certainly the most outrageous comedy I'd ever acted in. I usually do nice sophisticated comedies with Jane Fonda and people like that – gentlemanly roles. But here I am in Australia playing this bloody dinosaur with tattoos. It is just fantastic."[38]

Some years later he reflected, "Daddy-O had very definite facets of my own father. He was kind of a genuine ocker, a rigger who went out to the outback and put up water tanks and things like that, and he was very much like Daddy-O – not as bad, but he certainly had elements – and I enjoyed copying him in certain ways."[39]

It was an inspired decision to put him in the country's most potent sporting livery, the divisive black and white stripes of the Collingwood Footy Club. He exudes the sort of physicality that made Magpies like Des Tuddenham and Bob Rose dreaded and revered – not huge men, but physically assertive and capable of violence if required.[40] Daddy-O is a man we desire and fear in equal measure because Daddy-O will look after you if you do exactly what he says.

Mike Molloy evidently enjoyed photographing

Taylor's face, eyes showing feint threads of red, skin boiled raw as if he had spent his lifetime in Broken Hill rather than Beverly Hills. His ferocious masculinity and dictatorial control is the flint on which the other characters strike sparks.

And he is not just convincing, but intimidating – even for the audience. "I think the Aussie audience will laugh at Daddy-O because he's so horrible, but the other night they were terrified," he said in a Cannes interview. "I came out of the theatre and they were going 'Mon dieu'; they thought I was really a monster but I said, 'No, no, I'm nice!'"[41]

Elliott said it was a performance so large he had to fight to keep it under control. "The true base of what he was has been simmering away under the surface, boiling to get out, and this role came along and he just explodes on screen," Elliott said. "I usually tell the actors I am working with to turn it up a bit. Rod is the first actor I have worked with where I had to keep telling him to turn it down a bit. Once it was unleashed, the energy coming out of the man was just terrifying. I was there going, 'Down Rod, down, cool it baby.'[42]

"Working with Rod was a gift. I was walking through a huge video shop one day, my big casting secret trick, and stumbled across Hitchcock's *The Birds*.[43] There was Rod, aged thirty-three on the cover. He was now pushing seventy. Daddy-O was his first Aussie role in forty-odd years (excepting 1983's *On the Run*). To come back to the country at a certain age to play an Australian for the first time was a very big deal. He was very nervous of the script, very nervous about the whole thing really, but the shoot spoke for itself. He had a blast, and when he relaxed enough to go with the flow, he revelled in it. He scared the daylights out of us as Daddy-O, in fact. It was like this Australian rage just flowed out of him. There's a lot of Rod in the character, the boy from Harbord Beach in Sydney."[44] Elliott said there were great scenes omitted from the final version because Taylor's performance in them was "too dark, too heavy" for the film.

"We built this whole town with the greatest crew you can imagine," Taylor remembered. "We had a ball. 120 degrees in the shade but it was a funny, funny movie, and boy did I play this Aussie."[45]

Taylor's toughest moment came not in the brutal desert heat but in the Sydney studio. He was struggling badly with illness and injury prior to filming the unforgettable electrified tap-dance scene. "(I said) If you fill me full of pain pills and you trust me, I'll do anything to do it. And they said, you've got it."

The director knew he had to get it in one take. "He had to electric tap-dance on a steel bar, we had negative on the bar and positive on the tap shoes and let the sparks fly," Elliott said, speaking both literally and figuratively. "We did it real time, no special effects. Rod said he could only do it once so I got as many cameras as I could and Rod danced his heart out." In the process he badly damaged his hip, and required replacement surgery later that year.[46] The pain at the end of the scene was intense ("I fell off that bar and said 'Get me the fuck out of here'"[47]) but it provided one of the veteran's most indelible screen moments.

"I absolutely loved Daddy-O," Susie Porter said. "What an incredible actor. What an incredible man. Before any of the Aussies were doing it in America, there he was having the most incredible career, working with the most incredible people, and he had all these insane stories. He was such a gentleman. Just a dude."

A counterpoint to Taylor in almost every way was Johnathon Schaech. Taylor was a veteran; Schaech was an up-and-comer. Taylor was returning home; Schaech was an outsider in an alien country. Taylor's performance was a grace-note to a fine career; Schaech's uncertain outing damaged his prospects.

"So many times during takes I had flies crawling in

my mouth and out my ears," Schaech recalled. An earnest twenty-something from Maryland recently divorced from Christina Applegate, Schaech was further outside his comfort zone than anyone else on set. His star was in the ascendant, and an off-beat film working with the hot director of *Priscilla* had the potential to be mutually beneficial. "I remember I had several screenplays to choose from and I figured Steph coming off *Priscilla, Queen of the Desert* was a great gamble," Schaech said.

"But it was a gamble. The film title was *The Big Red* when I signed up. The next thing I knew, Steph was getting clearance to use famous Rodgers and Hammerstein tunes. The film took a creative turn right then and there. As preparation before the film, I started to gamble – playing poker and craps. Teddy took big chances, and I wanted to better understand the gambler's mentality. I was always looking for a certain edge for the role. I also rehearsed with Cameron Thor a great deal to get my comedic timing better, I prepared a Brooklyn accent with Jessica Drake and went to visit my cousins in Brooklyn, and I also watched a lot of John Travolta films. I was a very artistic fellow at the time and wanted to make great art but Steph didn't let me have a Brooklyn accent throughout, nor an outlandish hair style like Travolta in *Saturday Night Fever*, so I didn't get to play more of a character like I had planned. If I did, I think I would have been more pleased with my performance. I kinda was just the handsome loser."

"Sam Goldwyn Junior was hell-bent on getting a rising star," Elliott said. "Johnathon Schaech had just done the film which Tom Hanks directed (*That Thing You Do!*) and he was one of those 'rising stars'. In the end a gun was put to my head and I was told, 'I'm not having a has-been (like Matthew Broderick, Patrick Swayze or Luke Perry who we were toying with). You get a rising star or the film doesn't get made.' I saw some of Johnathon's work. Incredibly good-looking boy. Unbelievably, shockingly good looking. He wasn't quite what we had in mind but if it meant getting the film made...

"So I rang Tom Hanks' office and left a message asking about Johnathon, citing that before I gamble an entire movie on him I'd love some feedback. God bless Tom, he called back in about two minutes. 'Schaech's fabulous, great, wonderful.' I countered, 'Great. Now Tom – you're a comedian. Is he funny?' There was this enormous silence on the line before the answer: 'He can *learn* to be funny'. That still rates, to this day, as one of the weirdest decisions I've ever had to make. Hanks was telling me this boy wasn't naturally funny, and I was just about to make a comedy that needed an incredibly funny lead character. So it was a roll of the dice, and Johnathon came up snake eyes."

Elliott said that Schaech had his confidence rattled at the start of the shoot and only recovered it near the very end. The American had to wait in Sydney while Elliott recovered from illness, then his introduction to the film was travelling to ultra-remote Williams Creek with Barry Humphries and a skeleton crew. They filmed the scene in which Teddy gets petrol for his Kombi at Blind Wally's place.

Elliott remembered it this way: "Barry asks, 'Right Steph, what do you want?'

"'Well Barry, you're blind.'

"'Got it.' Turnover. Then the jaw-dropping moment where Barry grabs the petrol hose and starts slamming it into the side of the kombi saying, 'Where are ya, ya cunt?' That was classic Barry off piste. I'm crying with laughter, the crew are on the ground hysterical, and I suddenly realised Johnathon wasn't there. He wasn't even on set anymore. He'd run off and locked himself in a room. After a bit of TLC, I calmed him down. 'Why is that man funny? I'm the funny guy here.'

"I realised then and there that dear sweet Johnathon had no idea what was going on. He had been studying Laurel and Hardy movies because he thought that was how you did comedy. I will never blame him.

He took a real gamble on that role, and struggled terribly within the movie. He had a shit of a time because he's *not that funny*. He worked his guts out. It nearly killed him, making a film where everyone around him was naturally comedic. He was totally in the wrong movie, but that sort of worked for us in hindsight."

For his part, Schaech recalled by email, "I think it was my competitive nature in my acting. I hate being handicapped in a scene. And I just couldn't compete with the genius of Humphries. I was still finding Teddy at that time and trying to support Steph, but felt I was left hanging without the character tools I wanted or needed for Teddy. 'My goodness was Humphries hilarious!!!'"

"I remember Johnathon was upset and rang up his girlfriend in America," said Stan Yarramunua who played Young Lionel in the scene. "It was a bit hot and dry for him. It would have been tough to come from America to the outback."

Schaech had a "trillion-dollar smile," Elliott claimed, "but my god, what a bastard he was. When he was in a bad mood he would not smile, deliberately not smile. That was his big trick. He was a dark boy and he had a lot of demons. But all the baggage he brought to the film, the stranger in a strange land and his complete confusion, he did deliver a strong performance. This far down the track I now reckon Johnathon was worth it."[48]

The American seems to agree. "*Woop Woop* is still to this day my father's favourite film," Schaech said. "I make him laugh in it. I always admired Johnny Depp, and it was a Depp kinda movie. People ask if I'm any good at comedy and I just say, 'I have a whole bunch of comedies on my resume, but you'll never get to see them.' I wish we could make *Woop Woop 2*, because it is such a fun film. Today when someone says 'I loved *Welcome to Woop Woop*' it makes me smile. I think the movie is brilliant in its own way. And I also know the person who just said that probably saw it at 3 a.m. in the morning – because that's the only time it airs."

Making it

As a girl growing up in Wellington, New Zealand, Finola Dwyer's great passion was movies. She knew she wanted to work in the industry, trained as an editor and spent almost a decade honing her craft. In 1986 she secured an associate producer gig and left editing behind. In the early 1990s she moved to London and was a producer on the successful early-Beatles film *Backbeat*. In 1994, with the movie wrapped, she attended the Cannes Film Festival then holidayed in Italy. While there she read a proof copy of Douglas Kennedy's debut novel 'The Dead Heart'. "I laughed a lot, but there was also a great underlying tension," Dwyer recalled. "It was a great roller coaster of a story."[49] She shared the book with other *Backbeat* producers Stephen Woolley and Nik Powell of Scala. They put up the finance to option the book. Kennedy wrote an initial draft of a screenplay, before scriptwriter Michael Thomas – another member of the *Backbeat* team – was brought on board.

"It was just one of those books that reads like a film script," Nik Powell said. "It had the feel of an old opera where a woman had to sleep with the 'enemy' in order to save herself or her lover. In this case, Teddy has to sleep with a woman he doesn't love in order to buy the time to escape, and I loved the humour of it. It is wonderfully funny."[50]

At the 1995 British Academy of Film and Television Arts Awards, the BAFTA mandarins showcased their collective sense of humour by naming Hugh Grant as Best Actor for some listless swearing and excellent floppy hair in *Four Weddings and a Funeral*. Mike Newell, the man responsible for that manipulative trifle, was named Best Director ahead of co-nominated hacks Robert Zemeckis, Krzysztof Kieslowski and Quentin Tarantino. British border protection at its finest.

Stephan Elliott was at the ceremony. *The Adventures of Priscilla, Queen of the Desert* was nominated in six categories and won two of them. He was "pissed as a fart" and bemoaning the lack of decent scripts coming his way. Powell pulled one out of his bag called 'The Big Red'. It appealed, and he signed on. "I got a very dark script," Elliott said later. "It was very tough looking, quite a mean look at Australia and a lot of people thought it was very cool. On reading through, I took one look and I realised it was a black comedy and not big on the comedy, as was Douglas Kennedy's book."[51] He started messing with the script, looking for comic potential, bending it out of shape in cahoots with writer Thomas.

Then – film business. Sourcing finance. Auditioning actors. Scouting locations. Matching up geography and budgets and personnel and the calendar. Most of Elliott's casting choices came through. He barrelled up to Barry Humphries and had him committed to take part before you could say 'gladioli'. If preferred performers were hesitant, he employed his considerable charm. Dee Smart said, "I read (the script) and thought it was vile. I told (Stephan), how could this be funny? Then, after talking it through with him, I realised."[52] She became Krystal.

Coming off the back of an unheralded film that made approximately $80 million profit worldwide, Elliott looked like a good risk to investors. "We made it as an independent film, getting picked up in North America by the indie Samuel Goldwyn Company," Elliott said. "Sam Goldwyn [Jr.] is Hollywood royalty. The man himself sat me down, and said 'I've got no fucking idea what is happening with this script. No idea. However, I'm going to go with it because I trust *Priscilla*.'" The movie was bankrolled, the producers were bullish, pre-production went relatively smoothly, and it was ready for shooting at the end of winter in 1996.

Except Elliott was cudgelled by illness, and filming could not start until the end of spring. This would not have mattered in many locations, but the chosen site was Mount Ooraminna, south of Alice Springs, where temperatures soar as high as the wedge-tailed eagles. The site the filmmakers coveted was a massive meteorite crater a little further south called Gosses Bluff, but it was deemed too hard to access. It is used for the long shots that show the Woop Woop enclave from the outside.

"I went location scouting with the late Robin Clifton and producer Antonia Barnard," production designer Owen Paterson said. "We were trying to find a space that matched the description in the script of a crater. We thought if we could find a decent section of it we could get away with it. Robyn and I had previously worked down south of Alice Springs. We went past that place, visited the property owners at Mount Ooraminna and looked at their aerial maps. We saw that around the back of the mountain there was an area shaped like a hook. We photographed it, then flew over it next day in a helicopter. Beautiful country. We decided we would not find anywhere better, so we started to design the sets for that space."

The design and construction teams went to work in a natural elbow formed by the hills. (It was later turned into a ring of red cliffs via digital effects at Photon Stockman.) Piles of old tyres, a gargantuan stack of empty cans, a house constructed from bottles, threaded barbie dolls – no material was too tawdry for transformation. The set became one of the stars of the film. Andrew Urban visited Mount Ooraminna and reported: "There are 400 Cherry Ripes melting in a basket, countless tins of pineapple chunks, some of the props that range from regular kitsch to the surreal. All the interiors are dressed with bric a brac from hell in magnificent mess, and some of the costumes at the Christmas party include a dress made from the silvery innards of wine casks. A can mountain looms a dozen metres into the air: the cans are empty XXXX beer cans… Inside the beer can hillock is 500 metres of copper piping. Film sets are bizarre places, really."[53]

Paul Mercurio, cast as Midget, had previously shot another film south of Alice Springs, *Back of Beyond*. He reflected on the extraordinary experience of arriving on site and seeing the landscape transformed. "I was stunned when I walked onto the set for the first time," Mercurio said. "When I filmed there before it was pristine desert, quite a spiritual place. This time the town of Woop Woop was there, complete and mind-bending. Driving into the location at night with the set all lit up, I honestly felt like I was on the moon. It was a magical experience, one of those moments in film when you are taken away from what you understand reality to be."[54]

Casting was a prolonged but rewarding process. "We just had to find the right Angie and I knew who that Angie was," Elliott said. "I've been out to the outback too many times. I know these girls. Susie was dead on the money. Perfect. She's not outright pretty, but captivating and unbelievably ballsy. She's sunburned, freckled, tough as iron. She nailed that role completely. She and Rod walked away with the film.

"Richard Moir I worked with often when I was an AD. He was pretty crook at the time with Parkinson's disease, a long way into his illness. There were some days he'd get the shakes and say he just couldn't do it. I took him on knowing there would be issues. In the first couple of weeks he was struggling in front of other people, but once he caught the spirit of the shoot he let it go. He's shaking so badly in some scenes, but who cares? It worked. In the longer version of the film I gave him much more prominence as the town ratbag. He walked away from *Woop Woop* saying it was one of the greatest experiences of his life. It was also one of his last films.

"Mark Wilson played Duffy. You go into a casting session with an idea of what you want, then some stranger walks in, turns the dialogue on its head, does it so differently and you give him the role on the spot. Catching your director off guard can really land you a role. This kid did no prep. *He just was.* And probably still is. I have no idea if he even stayed in the business. It's a big problem when actors come in drowning in over-preparation. They're so locked into what they rehearsed in front of the mirror for the last few weeks they can't take any new direction.

"Bob Oxenbould, Moose, was a bank manager and I knew him very well socially. We used to put on Christmas pantos when I was a kid and he always stole the show. He and his wife Jan (Aunty Di) were not professional actors and that brought something intimate into *Woop Woop* for me. Con Demetriou – the muscle man – was maybe a misfire for some. Michael Thomas hates it. He rang screaming, 'What the fuck is the Muscle Mary doing there?' I said, 'It's funny.' Michael: 'It's not funny, he doesn't belong in Woop Woop.' And that's why it's funny."

On the first day of shooting the temperature on set topped the half-century. Celsius. The actors had a big air-conditioned bus dubbed the Honky Tonk Lady where they could retreat between takes, but the crew baked like a Christmas ham. Elliott was still suffering the after-effects of hepatitis. The combination of a punishing shooting schedule, the heat and the stress meant he lost more weight than he could afford. It also meant he could not party with other members of crew and cast, which might have saved his body if not his mind. The whole team drove back in to Alice Springs each night, and for some personnel the night-time recreational activities were as demanding as the daytime labour.

(Not everyone hit the booze. "In Williams Creek, me and Barry Humphries walked into the pub," Stan Yarramunua remembered. "All these blokes in singlets and shorts, you couldn't hear a pin drop. They just looked at us. Barry doesn't drink and neither do I, and they were trying to work out why the bloke who plays Les Patterson wasn't having a drink. Barry's an artist as well, so the both of us went for a little walk into the bush. He did some painting and I played the didgeridoo for him and his wife. We lay on the ground and above us was the Milky Way. That was really memorable.")

Hearts of Darkness: The Musical

The tempest that surrounded the making of *Apocalypse Now* was captured by Fax Bahr and George Hickenlooper in their 1991 documentary, *Hearts of Darkness: A Filmmaker's Apocalypse*. It is hard to imagine any shoot matching the turmoil of Coppola's attempt to make his masterwork in the Philippines with key personnel going rogue and a typhoon bearing down.

Be that as it may, there was a certain craziness at the core of the *Welcome to Woop Woop* experience also, abetted by a wild script, an insane set, a draining and difficult location, and bacchanalian revelry out of hours. Asked whether this was *Apocalypse Now* in the desert, Elliott laughed. "You know, it probably was. *Hearts of Darkness: The Musical*." It seems to be remembered by most as an amazing experience, albeit not one they are in a hurry to repeat. It is common for movie people to rave about special camaraderie on-set, but the bonds forged while making this film were a major factor in allowing a tough shoot to wrap on time.

"Working anywhere outside the CBD is difficult in my opinion, especially in Australia where costs are already very high and which rocket up into the stratosphere as soon as you have to move sets and crew/cast around the country," Co-Producer Antonia Barnard[55] said. "The actual experience of the NT was great – it was the location for my first job in feature films (*We of the Never Never*) and has always had a great fascination for me. The problems on a film like this are tenfold, but obvious. Distance from accommodation, food, water, facilities, airports, cars for hire, decent restaurants, the costs of which escalate when you go into remote areas, plus getting crew and cast in for short periods, difficult plane schedules, heat, weather, the need for hire cars for everyone, expensive hotels, expensive petrol – the list is endless.

"Weeks and weeks of construction work were halted precipitously when Stephan, turning slowly yellow by the day, was diagnosed with hepatitis only ten days before the shoot commenced. Everything came to a full stop while we tried to get a prognosis on his condition – estimates that ranged from six weeks to six months. But over all of this, the spectacular set in that red and rusty crater that forever defined the story and the location of the script will always stay in my mind's eye."

"I got hepatitis from a deep outback location recce which pushed us from a winter to a mid-summer shoot," Elliott said. "Put your finger dead centre of a map of Oz and that was the location. To get there from Alice (Springs) every day was a minimum sixty minute drive on a red dirt track one way. Once you've driven there and back, that's over two hours of your day gone in travel time, so when you can legally only work a ten-and-three-quarter hour day, we were shooting ourselves in the foot before we set off.

"First day it was fifty-two degrees on location. The outback was in deep drought and the heat was beyond unbearable, like nothing I had experienced before or have since. The sheer brutality of the whole situation was so bloody horrific, the crew kind of just went with it. When you're shooting in big city comfort like a studio and go into overtime, everybody starts complaining. Nothing is right: accommodation, per diems or dry cleaning bills. But this far out, in this much pain, it becomes quite a humbling experience. You become thankful for a simple glass of water. A strange camaraderie grew. I'd hear people saying, 'This is a fucking nightmare but what the fuck – let's keep drinking and soldier on.'

"We ran out of water a couple of days in and Antonia Barnard had to start bringing in an oil tanker of water. I'll never forget seeing how fast a crew could drink a tanker full of water. Then it got hotter. The cameras were not coping, we had 'action dogs' that had special little shoes custom-made for their paws because of the heat on the ground, and we were spraying extras down in desperation. I remember doing a scene where three extras collapsed from heat exhaustion mid shot. I was running like a mad thing but I looked like a stick of spaghetti, just disgusting," Elliott said.

Cinematographer Mike Molloy recalled that the working conditions were very uncomfortable, but "film people, especially crew, are pretty resilient. I've shot in everything from minus twenty degrees to plus fifty, in downpours and jungles. You just get on with it." The heat and dust caused major problems for the equipment however. After two days the camera operators realised that the snazzy Austrian Moviecams they were using were insufficiently robust, and they sent for replacement Panavision Gold cameras. "We had a guy from Panavision who slept during the day so he could spend all night cleaning the gear and getting the dust out ready for use the next day," Molloy said. "I remember one day out at Mount Ooraminna we were shooting exteriors, the temperatures were in the high forties and we got hit by this incredible dust storm. You just have to do your best.

"Even the interiors weren't easy. The pub's interior was back in the studio, if you could call it that – an old factory space at Homebush Bay. It was made of iron and as the day wore on, the heat built up, and the place expanded making cracking noises that drove the sound crew mental. The interior of Angie's bedroom was built in a corrugated iron shed in the showgrounds at Alice Springs. We shot that at night, but the residual heat, plus a few film lights, meant it was extremely hot. We would also have spectacular thunderstorms rolling over the West MacDonnells and that made the sound crew's job really tough too."

Molloy recalled that shooting began with the final scene of the film (excluding the amusing Paxton double-act after the credits) and it was a rough way to start. "On the first film I ever worked on (*Performance*) I said to the director Nic Roeg, 'What will we start with?' and he said, 'Something easy.' Make the first day easy. Make the first week achievable. Once you do that, the money people look at the progress report and think you're on budget and on time and leave you alone.

"But not in this case. It was the start of shooting, the weather was terrible, the heat was unbelievable, we were doing this damn scene at night with Rod Taylor, Dee, Susie and Johnathon. And a mining truck. We couldn't get the lights we needed up there in time. Stephan said, 'I just want the truck to be the light source,' and I thought, Christ. We did it on an airport runway and put supplementary lights on the mining truck as if they were work lights, but not enough were put on. We got out there in the pitch black, nobody knew each other, and we were two-thirds of a stop below what we needed, so they force developed the film and raised it by a stop, which is why it looks a bit grainy."

A far more satisfactory night scene was the one in which Paul Mercurio's character Midget tries to escape up the cliff-face and is shot down. "The sheer size of it was a challenge," Molloy said. "It was a huge thing to do in terms of lighting, and night lighting is always tricky. I had to fight hard to get a Musco light, which is fifteen lamps on a big cherry picker which extends upwards to about thirty metres. They were an American invention, and if you want to light a big area at night, park one of these things half a mile away and it's brilliant."

That remarkable scene was shot in real time. Mercurio only had a small timeframe in which to play the unfortunate hairdresser from Kununurra, so the crew worked throughout the night with five units shooting simultaneously. The dramatic fall down the cliff-face was performed by stunt coordinator Rocky McDonald. "Some fall," said Elliott admiringly.

"Another scene I was really pleased with was the one where they are watching the movies at night," Molloy said. "Nowadays you would just do it green screen and drop the images in, but we had to find a projector powerful enough to get an exposure on the screen. Someone found these wonderful slightly eccentric people who owned such a projector. We wanted to hire it but they said, 'No worries, we'll put it in the Kombi and drive up to Alice Springs, it'll be a good trip,' and so they did. We were shooting anamorphic, so the lenses were not quite as fast as conventional lenses. We shot a test, way open, and just got enough light. It was getting near time to shoot the big outdoor movie scene, we set the damn thing up, I took a polaroid to double-check the exposure and it was more than a stop underexposed.

"The man who owned the projector fiddled around with it and said it might be this or that. I was sweating; you've got 200 extras waiting in the wings, it could be a major hold-up. At the same time as this was happening we were doing the big shooting scene with Mercurio. I was actually up on the camera crane with Rod Taylor firing an elephant gun past my ear when someone gave the thumbs up and said a filter or something in the projector was cutting the light, that was fixed and it worked well indeed. It was just such a relief."

Construction coordinator Phil Worth broke his ankle and hobbled around the rocky set on crutches. Extras wilted. Some were fired. Local accountant Rowan Churches and his son Rouslun signed on as extras, but Rowan's services were terminated. "It was very hot and it took an hour to get from the rendezvous point to the site," he said. "After a while I grumbled about whether we were going to get paid for travelling to and from the site. I was apparently going to be in a dentist scene having my tooth pulled but then I was sacked and that scene must never have been shot or shot and cut." Flies were omnipresent, but the director ruled that true Woopites would not even notice them, so the actors were forbidden to brush them away while the cameras rolled.

A far bigger problem was that the film Elliott was shooting ("my outback Fellini, my outback John Waters film") did not seem to be the film that the backers expected. "The rushes started to come in, and this was not quite the movie *anybody* had in mind," Elliott said. "To be fair, having been so sick it probably looked like I may have gone completely off the rails. Add that to the heat, location and technical production problems, we were running behind within minutes. By day ten I got a tip off. The Americans, and all of Scala Productions were flying in to set from the UK. I was about to get fired. We were shooting the scene where Teddy wakes up in the chicken shed (next to a three-tonne pig called Chookie who worked tirelessly for blueberry muffins) when I spotted Finola leading the executive posse walking toward me with the rifles locked. This was it.

"I drew a big breath, excused myself, lay down in pig shit and rolled around. I punched a wall and threw myself into a wire fence until I was bleeding. I came back out of the chicken shed and went into overdrive, directing six shots at once covered in mud, shit, blood and tears. It was the performance of my career and saved my neck. How could they fire this thin man who was clearly killing himself to get this thing across the line?"

Elliott kept his job, and in the main he kept the cast and crew onside. An exception came when he filmed Dog Day, a cull where the kids of Woop Woop get to shoot their own and other people's dogs. "We fought for weeks with MGM over that one," Elliott sighed. "The town had to be littered with dead dogs for Dog Day but we didn't have the money to build dead dog 'dummies'. Colin Gibson came up with a genius solution. He did a deal with the local vet. If anyone brought a dog in to be put down and didn't want the remains, could we keep and freeze them? By the time we got to Dog Day, Colin had all these frozen dogs. But in the outrageous heat the frozen dogs would have lasted about five minutes before they'd melt. So someone came up with another genius idea of chain-sawing the dogs in half lengthways, putting the cut section away from camera, so for every one dog we'd get two dead dogs in the shot.

"It was about that point in time I had a cast rebellion. After Dog Day and the Woof Woof from Woop Woop scene, putting kangaroos through a giant mincer to make pet food, Susie Porter spat the dummy. A staunch animal activist, the day a truck full of dead roos arrived, I crossed the line when I asked her to shovel them with a pitchfork. Okay, we didn't actually kill them; we paid somebody else to do it. The problem was severe drought in Alice. Most of the local roos had already dropped dead on us, so poor old Antonia had to have them shipped in from South Australia. Then I made the cast start chopping them up with hacksaws. Susie was not happy."

Porter was a young Novocastrian, fairly new to films and playing a lead role in a major production, so it cannot have been easy for her to stand up to the director. "I remember waiting to do the shot and I had a pair of those bloody Dolce & Gabbana underpants on my head, I was in these platformed high heels, in a little room surrounded by dead kangaroos," she said. "I've always loved animals and these days I don't eat meat for ethical reasons. Obviously they weren't killed for the show, but I thought, this is quite bizarre. I also had a plastic bag over me, and I was just sweating it out in fifty degree heat."

If that was Porter's low point, the rest of the experience more than made up for it. "I think that was one of the happiest times I've ever had in my life," she said. "I was in the middle of the desert listening to *The Mission* soundtrack. It was like a travelling circus. I loved it. It was so outrageous. I remember in the Kombi van, doing stunts hitting the truck with an axe, and we took a break from that and I danced around in the desert and thought, 'What a great thing this is!'"

With her fair complexion it was a tough location for Porter, especially as she had to expose more skin than anyone else. "I think it was the first time I took my clothes off for a movie. I didn't understand the industry as well then. I thought, everyone does this, that's cool, I'll take my clothes off. It was no big thing. My genuine truth is that I'm not really comfortable with that. I'm certainly not ashamed of taking my clothes off, I'm not ashamed of what I did in *Woop Woop*, but I probably wouldn't do the same thing now."

Porter's other hurdle was finding a way to put across the stylised dialogue. "It was very difficult delivering some of the lines. I was always worried that I was being too big, but the character is so big. I had just got out of drama school, I was theatre-trained so I was terrified of being so big. I just had to go for it and not be half-hearted about it," she said.

There was nothing half-hearted about Maggie Kirkpatrick's effort either. She relished the bravura nature of the Ginger role, however lacking in subtlety it may have been, and sacrificed her locks for the cause. "It was entirely my idea to have my head shaved for Ginger's death scene," she said. "After seeing the pretend bald cap, I decided to go the whole way and have it all off. I also knew that this was what Stephan secretly wanted and he had been such a love on the shoot that it was no big deal for me to please him with this small gesture."

Ginger's funeral was the occasion for a rare burst of querulousness from Rod Taylor. Elliott recalls that Taylor was getting himself into character, ready to mourn his screen wife's passing, when costume designer Lizzy Gardiner handed him a salmon pink 1979 Safari suit to wear. "He didn't like it," Elliott said. "And he really didn't like it when the extras started to arrive in wedding dresses, Hawaiian barbecue outfits, ballet tutus. 'Jesus Steph! This is my wife's funeral, not a fucking circus!' I did the big Fellini sell and that calmed him down. A bit. Just as we roll camera for Rod's big emotional moment he starts screaming at me, 'Steph, I can handle surrealism. I can handle Fellini, but I can't handle the fucking clown!'

"I turn around and Lizzy has dressed this extra as a big top circus clown with three-foot shoes and blinking red nose. I had to have the clown removed for Rod while trying to keep a straight face. About three hours later, halfway through a difficult night shoot with a lot of pyrotechnics for the funeral, Rod starts screaming again. Into the back of the shot wanders the clown, now so drunk he could hardly walk. The poor bastard was banished into a set which luckily housed fifteen cases of hot Fourex beer (to be used as props) and obviously decided to drown his sorrows."

Despite occasional blips, the shoot was gruelling but good-humoured. Yarramunua said, "My favourite moment was when I jumped out of the van with one thong on and Johnathon said, 'Did you lose a shoe Lionel?' and I said, 'Nah brother, I found one.' I remember doing the bus trip, seeing the Aboriginal people there, the way they were living. It was good to be back in that country. It was a real Aussie movie."

Kirkpatrick confirmed that, "the atmosphere was better than on other shoots where conditions were more luxurious. There was so much camaraderie among cast and crew. So much laughter! I think we all did a damn good job, entering into the spirit of fun that Stephan generated during that wonderful, mad time. The hardships of the day were certainly relieved by cool, comfortable hotel surroundings at night and copious cans of VB by the pool."

"Oh, there was a lot of partying," Porter agreed. "We were in Alice Springs and we took over the place.

I remember I had done a night shoot, I took a couple of sleeping tablets so I could sleep during the day, but some of the cast and crew just broke down my door and came in and grabbed me and said, 'You're partying'. And away we went. We had the best fun ever. I've still got mates that became good friends because of that movie."

One person not partying was the team's fearless leader. "I look at the photos now and I'm just skin and bone after being sick for so many months," Elliott said. "By shoot I still couldn't eat properly or drink properly, I was rake thin, on a very strict diet, and drinking booze was a no-no. The rest of the crew didn't have the same excuse, and once the pub and mini-bar doors opened, it was just absolute carnage. The shoot was beyond physically exhausting but I'd go back to my hotel room each night, be given a lettuce leaf and told to go to bed early. Then I'd lie there listening to absolute bacchanalia going on in the other hotel rooms."

Elliott was still capable of having some fun, however. "I'd earmarked the 'pork sword' truck driver cameo but Finola Dwyer refused to let me do it. 'This film's not all about *you*.' And to be fair she had been working on *Woop Woop* for about seven years and there I was hijacking it. So while we were shooting the giant kangaroo on a blue screen, I snuck outside with the second camera, climbed in the cabin of the grip's truck and knocked it off in a couple of minutes without anybody knowing. She never knew about my cameo until she saw the first assembly.

"Another swiftie I pulled on Finola was the love scene where Teddy cuts Krystal in half as a magic trick in the Woop Woop pub. It was end of shoot, we had just sailed into overtime and the production kitty was almost empty. Finola had decided the scene should be cut and never shot. I got the call three minutes before wrap. She was very sad but the decision was made. I agreed, hung up and screamed at the crew, 'Get all the props on the pool table, put the zooms on the three cameras and start shooting. We're going to roll it until they physically came out here and pull the plug.' And the *Woop Woop* cast and crew being what it had now become, they went into overdrive like naughty school children. By the time Finola and Antonia arrived an hour later, I had fourteen sets in the can. The scene did make the final cut."

Most memories of the movie's making focus on the outback experience. "Shooting in the desert humbles crews," Elliott said. "Crews are really, really, really, really quiet out there." However there were also memorable moments in other locations. Porter's topless sprint in and out of the surf occurred at Dee Why, standing in for a West Australian beach. The last days of the shoot were with a small crew in the central desert, and provided the early scenes on the road with Teddy and Angie. Elliott has noted that Schaech's performance is perceptibly more comfortable in these scenes.

The film's opening, ostensibly in wintertime New York, was largely filmed in the back streets of Sydney suburb Surry Hills in high summer, with foam scattered on the ground to look like snow. It is cleverly intercut with footage shot by a New York unit, "running through Times Square without a permit". Rachel Griffiths effortlessly steals this, her only scene. Her character Sylvia is accused of being a prostitute but Teddy says that she is an exotic dancer. "I am classically trained," she drawls. When Sylvia pulls out a gun and starts firing wildly, she offers the neat justification, "This is America, Teddy. I can shoot who the hell I like."

An unexpected nuisance in post-production was a claim by Disney that the title originally appended to the project, 'The Big Red', was too similar to *Big Red*, the name of their 1962 movie with Walter Pidgeon, an orphan and a lovable Irish Setter. Some audiences may have been confused as to which film was which, but astute types would have picked up that the expression 'Fuck me dead' is used eight times in the latter film and not once in the 1962 delight. Regardless, a new and better title was formulated – a pungent, memorable title which, for whatever reason, was generally hated.

Cannes

The biggest dance in world cinema is Festival de Cannes, the annual coming out ball for the globe's brightest filmmakers. The hedonistic French glamourfest and Puckish, quixotic Elliott were a natural fit; after all, he had the Cannes audience doing a can-can of delight when *The Adventures of Priscilla, Queen of the Desert* was given a special Midnight Screening at the 1994 festival. Acclaim was immediate, the after-party was legendary and Elliott was a genius.

Flash forward to 13 May 1997. On the strength of *Priscilla*'s spectacular debut, Elliott was convinced to accept a special Hors Concours screening at the festival for *Welcome to Woop Woop*. The Cannes selection committee had not seen the film – and it was far from finished. The first draft was stitched together but the director estimated that he was about one-and-a-half months away from having a completed version. This was roughly the amount of time that hepatitis had stolen from the production prior to the commencement of shooting, days he never managed to claw back.

"My first instinct was to pass," Elliott recollected. "But festival head Gilles Jacob pressed all the right buttons: 'Coppola screened *Apocalypse Now* – my favourite film – unfinished at Cannes and won the Palme d'Or.' My eyes grew bigger than my stomach."

That stomach was churning in the lead-up when Elliott knew he was going to show a film that was not yet ready to be seen. "I got to first draft with it, and if I had another six weeks of cutting time I would have found a way through. You do a first draft of a script or book, you naturally give it some time, come back after some soul searching and pondering, and the pieces start to gel. We had the first draft of *Woop Woop*, and instead of pondering, we took it on a nice holiday to the French Riviera and screened it before the most judgmental audience on earth."

The situation was complicated by the film acquiring a new owner when Goldwyn's boutique company was bought out by monolithic MGM. "Even though Sam was backing *Woop Woop* financially and didn't understand anything about the film – making his time in the cutting room a nightmare – when he suddenly disappeared from the picture and we woke up one morning with a major American studio as the owner, that was not how this film was supposed to be made," Elliott said. "I envisaged it as a kind of surrealist, out-on-a-limb smaller independent gamble."

Gambling was in the air. MGM's money men sniffed the Cannes breeze and intuited that they had lucked into a massive hit. Prior to the Hors Concours unveiling they tore up the pre-sales agreements and purchased world rights. The MGM plunge meant that a wickedly subversive independent film was suddenly loaded with crazy expectations of multiplex triumph. "MGM took over the entire movie at Cannes, and that ultimately was the death of it," the director remembered. "The pre-sales on the back of *Priscilla* were so strong that I'm told *Woop Woop* was in profit before the film rolled through the gate. However, on the night before the screening in Cannes, the buzz was so strong, MGM ripped up every existing sales contract and bought the world. The pressure on a film that wasn't finished was excruciating."

If the screening had been a success, this could have worked in everybody's favour. But it was anything but. "Cannes was a disaster," Michael Thomas said. "The film wasn't finished, there was a terrible unfunny bad-tempered voiceover, all the Korean buyers were barking at their phones. The seats in the Grand Palais are sprung;

when you get up they hit the back with a clap. All we could hear was these clapping seats."

Co-Producer Antonia Barnard said, "The first time I saw it screened to a public audience was as a work in progress in Cannes. The silence at the end of the screening was devastating – especially as Stephan had received a 15 minute standing ovation for *Priscilla*. I don't feel that you can go into a film without anticipating that the end product will be a huge hit, or a little hit, or at the very least an arthouse hit, and with a project such as this, the gamble was whether it would catch on. Why would you put so much into a project if you thought it was going to fail? Stephan was a director with a major profile after *Priscilla* and the company which developed the script in London (Scala Productions) also had a big profile. It was always a gamble because of its outrageous premise and the 'musical' style of the film but when it didn't take the world by storm it was, obviously, disappointing."

(Satirical newspaper The Chaser jibed, "The first financier to see the cut of Stephan Elliott's Welcome to Woop Woop must have felt the strange calm that enveloped kamikaze pilots getting into the cockpit."[56])

Susie Porter called the Cannes experience, "an absolute doozy". There are various stories told of the get-together in the aftermath of the screening but few are printable. A three-word phrase used by several who attended the event sums it up: 'Worst. Party. Ever.' The hangover was worse. "No-one would look at me at my own afterparty, then we woke up the next day with a disastrous result," Elliott said. "The day after the screening no-one wanted to touch us with a 40 foot pole, and that was the beginning of the end of *Woop Woop*."

Two days later, Liberation film critic Élisabeth Lebovici reported to her French readers on the screening and the film itself in a piece titled 'Woop Woop flounders in the desert'. She reported that the dress code for the screening was to "put yourself on your 31, Australian style" ('put yourself on your 31' is a French expression equivalent to 'put on the ritz') then opined, "You would be hard placed to judge whether the outfits worn on Tuesday night actually met this recommendation, so much did the film take Australia to a level of visual and audio exasperation way past 31 on the Richter scale... the plot is fairly limp and the laughs infrequent, so much does the film make a show of its flagrant desire to make spectators as hysterical as its set designer."[57]

Noël Herpe was a little more positive in Positif. He wrote that, "Stephan Elliott reproduces here the techniques that made *Priscilla, Queen of the Desert* a hit, by imagining a totally artificial backwater where puppets possessed by a sweet delirium bustle about".[58] *"...en imaginant un bout du monde totalement artificiel et où s'agitent des marionnettes en proie à un doux délire."* These are likely the most beautiful words ever written about the film. Yes, Herpe might be criticising the movie as contrived – but they are puppets, it is an artificial backwater, and they are definitely possessed by delirium, be it sweet or otherwise.

Whatever. By that point critics could have written sonnets to rival Shakespeare or songs to outshine Solomon. It would have made no difference, because no-one was listening. The important minds had been made up already. The film was garbage.

Backlash

Elliott went to work with his editors, weaving and snipping, trying different ways, testing different angles, removing approximately twenty-four minutes of material. It was at this point that others started messing with his vision. The overall tone shifted closer to the apocalyptic bleakness of the book. The dictates of the box-office came into play, and he was required to compromise. There were fights over control. He lost the privilege of final cut. The project was batted about by different film company bureaucrats, trying to edit up an acceptable version for theatrical release without knowing what the film was supposed to be.

"The massacre in the cutting room began," Elliott said. "There's a terrific moment when Rod gives this great monologue on why you should live and die a Woop Woopite. There's a tracking shot in the scene which for me is the defining moment of the movie. Rod spins straight to camera and he says 'It's too fucking dry, it's too fucking hot, but it's ours. *It's Australia.* And I think that's something worth fighting for. Hands up those of youse who think it's worth a fight?'

"That's the original script line but that's not what's in the film. What's left in the finished product is a cheap, weird special effect that says something completely different. And it sums up exactly where we were all standing at the time. Sam Goldwyn starts screaming, 'What's he talking about Australia for? Shouldn't he say "It's Woop Woop"? Cut it out.' 'Sam, Woop Woop is the big metaphor for Australia. It's also a single shot and I don't have any alternative coverage for an overdub'. Sam shoots back, 'Do what you're told or I'm cutting the whole scene out.' So if you look at the shot today, as it gets up to that point in the line, instead of saying, 'It's Australia' you'll suddenly see a bad CGI effect of somebody else's lips done on a video handycam saying, 'It's Woop Woop'. I don't even think it's Rod's voice. Some guy in the SFX house. That single line is why I made the movie, and even that was compromised."

The proposed Australian release date of 8 January 1998 came and went. So did the next planned date, in April. There was unanticipated publicity prior to release when Adelaide City Council banned one of the film's posters which showed Angie on her back with her legs wide part and Teddy in between them. The Federation Of Australian Commercial Television Stations refused to show the first trailer due to offensive dialogue, taking particular dislike to Porter's line, 'Part my beef curtains.'[59]

It finally slid onto the screen in August that year. It was condemned before it even opened. Adrian Martin began his review in 'The Age' with, "There are few Australian films that arrive with such a forbidding 'word of mouth' as *Welcome to Woop Woop*. I have already been told by numerous sources it is very possibly the worst Australian feature ever made."[60] It opened in the same week as another local film, the full-on *Head On*. Elliott noted the poor timing, saying, "This industry is not big enough to support two Australian films competing with each other." It reached North America on 13 November 1998, showed on just five screens in the USA, and grossed a paltry $19,812 on opening weekend.

The director manfully took on some PR duties, doing promotional interviews for a film that no longer felt like his own. His best quip was that, "Woop Woop is the arse end of the world, and this young American is just passing through it." That marketing pitch had more zip than his longer version: "It's blowing one last big kiss goodbye to the mass of old Australian culture which is disappearing: 50s, 40s, 60s culture which is just about to go...there is beer guzzling, there is sexism, you name it, it still exists out there, but slowly the city is trying to pretend that it doesn't. It will eventually disappear; it is disappearing. This is my homage, my goodbye to a great piece of Australian culture that I think is just terrific."[61]

Interviewed in the US, he described it as "a musical version of *Deliverance*" which showed the flip-side of the *Priscilla* fantasy of outback Australia. "It was very hard out in the desert, making *Priscilla*, and we spent a lot of time covering up the harsh conditions. That was something I wanted to capture with *Woop Woop*. I thought, I've done the fluffy version, but it's a really tough life out there."[62]

None of his spruiking cut through. The flip-side of the feted *Priscilla* was condemned to an equally flip-side fate. "The finished film is a long series of compromises for a nice but clearly confused old American geezer and a major US movie studio which had absolutely no idea what the film was about," Elliott reflected. "They chopped it down into – well – something they couldn't put their fingers on. The closest description I got was 'a Monty Python film' which it isn't. I would love to raise the money and put it back together one day. The footage is all there, because I kept everything. On previous films I dumped the lot in fits of rage. Not this puppy. It's all in storage. I just have to find the finance. As she stands, I'm extremely happy with the movie's overall look – if not too happy with the clunky sound mix. But the look, and more importantly, the tone was right, and that pissed a lot of people off. Mission accomplished. Everyone wanted me to make *Priscilla 2*, and in a way I did, but I flipped it. It's incredibly smart. In the long cut, it was spelled out very clearly. I can still see little glimpses of what it is trying to say, which was something unique. There are snippets and clues, even a couple of real gems left behind, but ultimately it was the second baby (after *Frauds*) that got taken away from me, being forced through a machine that never let it out."

Some people involved with the movie are convinced that the vituperative reviews and disproportionate backlash damaged their careers.

Primarily Johnathon Schaech. "Looking back, in all honesty this film cost me a true shot at stardom," he reflected. "I had so many films and opportunities to choose from at the time. I was on the cover of Vanity Fair as one of the next leading men of Hollywood, opposite Will Smith/Matthew McConaughey/Leo DiCaprio etcetera. MGM shut the picture down at some point. No-one ever really told me what happened. I was put on the shit list and I think the movie was only screened in West Hollywood where they handed the audience members men's underwear with 'Welcome to Woop Woop' written on them. Either the studio didn't like the movie or they felt me and Steph couldn't open to a wider audience. I believe we could have at the time, given the chance.

"But the truth is, I made two choices that ended up shutting down (temporarily) my leading man days: *Welcome to Woop Woop*, and *Finding Graceland* with Harvey Keitel and Bridget Fonda – two movies I love but very few people have seen. I chose those two films because I guess I wanted to be an indie guy, like a Johnny Depp making offbeat character-driven stories, when I should have been doing studio features. I didn't know any better and only until now do I care," he said.

Cinematographer Mike Molloy also felt targeted. "I was very disappointed with the critical response," he said. "I think it affected my chances of getting other movies in Australia, it was so badly received."

Emerging star Susie Porter had a different take, shaped by her own experience. In the five years after *Welcome to Woop Woop* she was in eleven films, often as a lead, and four television shows. "I don't think any one film has the power to wreck a career," she said. "I think that is putting too much power to a film that not too many people saw. It was a film we expected to do better, and we all learned a lesson in reality. That's my view, and I can laugh about it now, but at the time it was like – wow. It was my first experience of people being really nasty."

Make no mistake: when it comes to knocking, Australians are world class. Consistent, energetic, dedicated. Savants of the bagging game. After Cannes and before release, *Welcome to Woop Woop* started to get a smell about it. Stephan Elliott needed to be taken down a peg or five. "They never gave it a chance, plus Steph purposely offended Aussies (in a funny way) as much as he could have," Schaech said.

Sure enough, the local critics gleefully took up the challenge to find more damning ways of saying the film was a turkey. No sledge was too strong. When 'Senses of Cinema' released its list of nominations for Worst Film of the Millennium, *Welcome to Woop Woop* was included.[63] The worst film ever made, anywhere – flippant or not, that is some label.

"The reviews in Australia were bitchy," said Michael Thomas. "We hit a sore point with a nine-pound hammer. They all complained Australia isn't like that any more. Nobody wants to recall with love and pride the brief period before the big boom in the sixties when the country actually had a culture, an ethos all its own, i.e. the world's first and only egalitarian white society, rooted in the sins of our ancestors and hatched in the pub, where you rode up front in the cab and there were no tall poppies etcetera. Australia Nouveau don't like to be reminded of those pre-tapas pre-cappuccino days when we all ate meat pies and Minties. For me and Steph, and gloriously for Rod T too, they are Eden. Nobody got the joke.

"Clearly to me, Australia doesn't go to Australian movies. They are up there with the dumbest consumers on the planet. The bright young things in the local press spend all their time talking about the movie that they think you should be making, like they know more about it than you do."[64]

Typical of the lusty energy some critics put into demolishing the movie was the review by Clark Forbes in the 'Sunday Herald-Sun'. He claimed that Elliott had followed the acclaimed *Priscilla* with, "a boring bit of bush grunge. In doing so, Elliott suggests he is a one-hit wonder, a bloke who has been standing in the sun too long without a hat...Some reviewers, who clearly have not been north of Brunswick, are praising this as a vicious parody of the Aussie cultural cringe. What cringe?...No cringe there, son. Just no point. What on earth is this all about? Yes, it is crude, but so what? Yes, it is over the top, but no more than half a dozen other Australian films that have placed a child in charge of the pie stall. But it can not escape the charge that it is as dreary as a wet day in Hobart. It sucks."[65]

"The political climate here in Australia was Pauline Hanson, so it was politically not the right time for the film," mused Susie Porter. "There was a reaction against looking at Aussies as bogans, racists, backwards. When you look at what makes movies successful, certainly it is about elements of stories coming together, but it is also about timing and something magical in the universe. There are not that many brilliant films. Lots of movies get made, all the marketing goes on, but most don't put bums on seats. Sometimes they are just missing that extra magical element."

Then the international critics started to have their say, and Australians knew that was not good. A lousy local film might be forgotten or forgiven over time, even if its director is an uppity motormouth overdue for a dose of humility – but embarrassing Australia in front of our sophisticated big brother, the USA? Unforgiveable.

Stephen Holden, New York Times: "this desperately unfunny farce...an incoherent mess of thrown-together scenes heaping scorn and ridicule on the Australian equivalent of Dogpatch ...operates on the principle that indiscriminate camp silliness can carry a movie."[66]

Lisa Schwarzbaum, Entertainment Weekly: "unrelentingly heavy whimsy makes for royal tedium, and Elliott's broad caricature of outback eccentricities comes across as more crude (even cruel) than charming."[67]

Edward Guthmann, San Francisco Chronicle: "pointless…Basically a live-action adventure cartoon."[68]

Christine James, Box Office: "Elliott has successfully created an environment so vile that it appropriately evokes the direness of escape. But unfortunately, the audience will also want to escape, long before the credits roll."[69]

The amateurs were eager to go the knuckle, too. The indispensable IMDB includes contributor reviews.[70] Let's hear it, voice of the people:

Tresy Kilbourne: "an overlong, meandering plot; thinly drawn characters and a general infantilism of vision…maybe it's just a gay thing, but I don't think camp works when it's a primary aesthetic mode."

Mappy the Mouse: "an intrinsically bad film"

cole_mars: "I remember seen (sic) this horrific film in New York…After about 30 minutes I was in pain, I had contortions all over my body, the garbage that was shown on the screen was making me puke, people around me were also in disgust."

Aussie Stud: "this garbage that not only bruises Australia's reputation and appearance, but makes a mockery of everything labelled 'Australian'…I was astounded and flabbergasted at how awful this movie was… trust me folks – this movie definitely does NOT represent ALL of Australia."

Cameron Koo: "a miscarriage of intended mirth that is about as whimsical as having battery acid poured over your genitals. Thomas' cringing dialogue could have been written by root vegetables and Elliott's slipshod direction seemed to drift between comatose and cataleptic…I candidly advocate that you avoid 'Welcome To Woop Woop' like you would a syphilis-spitting camel."

A prolific blogger who chooses to be known only as Convict Wally saw the movie as endangering the whole Australian film industry, because it broke trust between filmmakers and the audience: "Stephan Elliott's mean spirited attempt to portray the heart of Australian culture as racist, sexist, crass and revolving around excessive drinking...For Elliott, it seems watching people smile covered in kangaroo blood, or shoot their pets, is the ideal of modern humour. *Welcome to Woop Woop* flopped. The violence was too foul to be funny, and the 'jokes' were just stupid or insulting...(Australian filmgoers) retained their love of Australia, but reserved scorn for the subculture entrusted to tell Australian stories in film."[71] Ah yes – that uniform subculture of Australian film directors. As similar and interchangeable as Besser blocks. Stephan Elliott, Ana Kokkinos, Rolf de Heer, Brian Trenchard-Smith, Tony Ayres, George Miller, Tracey Moffatt, Cate Shortland, Greg McLean, peas in a pod the lot of 'em.

"The critical response hurt like hell at the time, but when you're as battle weary as I am now, you can look back and laugh," Elliott said. "Daryl Somers was 'appalled', refused to do the scheduled *Woop Woop* promotion on *Hey Hey It's Saturday* – his 'crazy show' for little old ladies in 1950s Blackpool – because he found the film 'disgusting'. What a cunt. Daryl Somers hated it and One Nation loved it. It should have been the other way around. It all went topsy-turvy. The wrong people were getting the joke. A One Nation spokesman[72] said it was a great movie, exactly what Australia needs at the moment, and I'm banging my head against the wall thinking, 'You are the fucking joke, you moron.'"

The film was supported by a few Australian critics. On *The Movie Show,* David Stratton opined that, "Elliott's film is very light on plot, but if you're not offended by these outrageous characters, there's plenty to enjoy in this well-made film, and the frequent juxtaposition of romantic songs from those wonderful old musicals and the far from romantic denizens of Woop Woop makes for some great moments of hilarity. Best of all is Rod Taylor, an inspired piece of casting as Daddy-O, the patriarch of Woop Woop – he's terrifically funny."[73]

Urban Cinefile's Andrew L. Urban cautioned against comparisons to the Bazza McKenzie films because, "Elliott is far more subversive. In particular, he adds a surreal element with the frequent, inappropriate use of Rodgers & Hammerstein in all the 'wrong' places at all the 'wrong' times. Some of the humour in the film is rather fast and/or sophisticated, though, despite appearances... Great photography, grotesquely kitsch but fitting production design and these truly bizarre elements – plus the memorable characters – will all no doubt help make it at least a cult classic, an ode to Australian sensibilities that have now almost vanished."

Tom Ryan was careful with his praise in The Sunday Age, and took a passing swipe at what he considered racism and sexism in Elliott's previous feature, *Priscilla*, but his commentary was generally positive. "The broadside directed at Australian ways by *Welcome To Woop Woop* might stretch our sense of humor a tad, but its satire is certainly very funny. And assured. If you can imagine *The Hills Have Eyes* set to a Rodgers and Hammerstein score, then you're on the way to appreciating the pulpy appeal of Stephan Elliott's new film...(W)hile the satirical jibes come thick and fast, there's nothing offensive about *Welcome To Woop Woop* (unless what 'The Advocate', the Catholic one, used to condemn as 'snatches of nudity' and the 'occasional profanity' sends you racing to the confessional or the pulpit)."[74]

There was some measure of approval in Adrian Martin's review: "...a welcome consistency of tone and energy...a wild, vulgar romp through popular myths of Australian nationalism and identity...gruesomely fascinating...Woop Woop constantly threatens to become a grandly incoherent mess. But it is when we get to the central topic of the film – its attitudes to a changing Australia – that the feathers really start flying...More and more, it presents 'old' Australia – patriarchal, mono-cultural, nostalgic, homophobic – as a fascistic abomination...a way of life that has reached its historical use-by date."[75]

Elliott said, "I think there was only one reviewer in the whole world who got it on release, although some Scottish newspaper review said, 'This is as close as I've seen to a Fellini film in 30 years.'"

The review which the director felt best critiqued his film was by veteran Todd McCarthy in 'Variety' a fortnight after the screening in Cannes. "I respect his opinion very much," Elliott said. "His take was, you get the feeling *Woop Woop* is some kind of private joke and Elliott's not letting us in. He was basically saying we didn't give enough tools to understand what was going on in the cut-down version. Very, very astute."

McCarthy called it, "a uniquely off-the-wall comedy that has the nature of an elaborate private joke played out on a lavish scale," and "highly peculiar rather than outright funny". McCarthy predicted it would, "fascinate and entertain those who manage to tune into (Elliott's) strange wavelength" but that "B.O. prospects look dicey", particularly because Australians may feel insulted. He concluded that, "Connoisseurs of oddball cultural phenomena will be endlessly engrossed; the majority will be left gaping in bewilderment."[76]

The look

In *Weekend*, Jean-Luc Godard inserted a card into the opening titles that translates as, 'A film found on the scrapheap'. Insert your own title card for Welcome to Woop Woop. A film made on a scrapheap? A film made from a scrapheap? A film destined for the scrapheap? All apply. Australia was founded as a scrapheap, a dump for human refuse from too-full England. Our culture was a bricolage of that which was brought here, that which was already here, and that which grew here. A culture of scraps, heaped together. We can own that if we choose. It need not be a source of shame.

The investment of care, flair and effort in the way the film looks paid big dividends. Likewise the construction of a skewiff township in the desert, a crazy folly that proved worthwhile. Traditional Owners were consulted about sacred sites; the production was close to, but not actually on, sacred country. The township was built on sand (suggesting ignorance of the classic Sunday School song[77]) and subject to fierce storms. Despite this, Finola Dwyer remembered her excitement at seeing the township grow on each pre-shoot visit.

Owen Paterson, Lizzy Gardiner and Elliott developed a bleached-out colour scheme. "'The wardrobe department used some primary colours to give the place a little bit of light and I used a couple of green and red lights on the pub, giving that garish 1950s feel, but colour is very limited in the whole film," production designer Paterson said.

"Stephan had this amazing idea of an Australian country town with a pub, church, cinema, houses, and we made a lot of it from found materials. They were cool things to draw and sketch and design. As a designer the criteria I was given was to create this asbestos town, officially abandoned, where people had either come back or stayed and refused to leave. It is like form following function. We realized that no-one in the town would have had any money for thirty years so it was a matter of building it so it would look like it's falling apart.

"Colin Gibson, the art director, did an amazing job of getting the pieces built. The cinema roof was to be like Grauman's Chinese Theatre in Hollywood, but rather than using curved tiles we used a whole lot of beer cans from Castlemaine Fourex which gave us these great yellow and red colours. We had the watchtower built with a big spotlight, and shacks that were a bit like a hippy commune but that still worked in a conservative town," Paterson said.

"We took our design inspiration from magazines and books of older Australia. Of course, we were in some of the most amazing land in the world. Most of the interiors were built back in Sydney and shot at studios out near where the Olympic Stadium was built. I remember the interior of the pub, half of it was falling down, there was a slippery slide embedded in the stair case, the bar had a metal top so Rod Taylor could do a tap dance down it with sparks flying out like an arc welder. A lot of this was just great ideas coming out of Steph."

Gardiner's buying team spared the credit card and scavenged thirty-five bags of old garments and fabrics from the tip. "I wanted to make the characters almost reptilian so that they would disappear into the red dust, which was very challenging," Gardiner said. "We had to dye the entire wardrobe terra cotta.

"The ultimate challenge is to create wardrobe so that as soon as the audience sees the character they have a sense of some kind of history, present and even future. The touchstone for Teddy was a 1990s version of John Travolta's character in *Saturday Night Fever*. Angie was based on a Barbie doll. She's just ridiculously sexy."[78]

Incongruities abound, but Elliott said, "To my surprise, punters have slowly put the puzzle together over the years. I would have preferred to have spelled it all out, but maybe you prefer puzzle? Example: 1987, big rains had come down in a small town called Nyngan. The place was underwater. The council asked the whole country to donate everything you've got spare for the Nyngan Flood Appeal. So my girlfriend [Rebel Penfold-Russell] grabs an old, very expensive Valentino dress she no longer wears and talks me into coming to Sydney Showgrounds to give to the flood relief. There, in a giant Garbage Day-like pile, hundreds of wedding dresses, designer gowns, platform shoes and vertical grills. For all these people drowning under twenty feet of water. I never got that image out of my mind – an outback town dressed in all this unwanted shit.

"Cut to a pivotal scene in *Woop Woop* where Rod drives up in the big truck and he screams, 'The rain's come down in Marble Bar', an Aussie classic, and empties the weirdest assortment of clothing from a flood appeal. The most inappropriate crap on earth. From that point onwards the film goes into its Fellini stage. The good people of Woop Woop dress in all these weird leftovers. But the Americans made me take the scene out. The execs just didn't get it, so it went. It's funny to look at the film now, how fucking bizarre the clothes get with no explanation as to why," Elliott said.

"The visual style we used when shooting was very very wide shots to very very close ups. You're always thinking about rhythm. In the edit, three-quarters of the way through there is a tonal change, more surrealist, with a lot of dissolves. The editor, Martin Walsh, didn't like dissolves so we got into a huge punch-up and I had to do them on my own.

"Mick Molloy's visual take was interesting. When you're out in really harsh sunlight mid-desert and you wander into a shack, it's pitch black until your eyes adjust.

That's the moment he was trying to create, the seconds before your eyes adjust. Dark places with light fighting to get through small cracks in a leaky wall."

"I thought the film called for a really saturated look, and that's what I gave it," Molloy said. "Back in London Stephan did another print, lighter and washed out. I said, 'Christ, that's flat, it looks terrible.' He said, 'I thought the print you did was a bit chocolate boxy.' I said, 'I think it looks better my way,' and in the end he agreed.

"Owen Paterson did an amazing job. A good production designer can make the cameraman's job much easier because a good production design gives you opportunities to light. When there is that sort of collaboration, everybody wins. Owen did the wonderful exterior and interiors. I said, 'You did a hell of a job.' He said, 'Oh, I was nickel and dimed like crazy. If only there was some more money – if only I could have done a supermarket.' Can you imagine what his Woop Woop supermarket would have been like? That would really have been something to see!"

Visual richness was paramount, from a fancy shot of the Milky Way reflected in a dead kangaroo's eyeball, to the construction of the Founding Fathers Club as a bastardised homage to Russell Drysdale's iconic pubs. The bizarre costumes range from Duffy's patterned pyjamas to a Christmas dress made out of wine-cask bladders. The camera captures every magnificent mark on Daddy-O's face, the personification of old Australia. Teddy is given an array of garb to wear, often unhappily, the best of which is the leather outfit he wears when he arrives in the outback: a transplanted shiny-scaled lizard in the middle of a foreign desert. No detail is too small for fun; there are fan pics of Bob Rogers and John Laws sticky-taped in Reggie's radio booth, and the drapes in the back of the Kombi are made of fabric printed with t-bones, a sly pun on the notorious 'beef curtains'. White cockatoos are used as a linking device: seen in a New York alley, and over the Chrysler building, and above the desert, and on Krystal's shoulder, and in the final scene after the credits. Angie says, "I'm as happy as a pig in shit," then a few minutes of screen time later Teddy is literally lying with a pig in shit. (Not so happily.)

When shooting finished at Mount Ooraminna, the bean-counters worked out that striking the set and removing it would cost too much. Instead the entire set was torched. Elliott called it "a glorious day". It might have been some sort of metaphor.

The sound

The movie's music is eclectic. Of course. Classic show tunes are afforded hip reinterpretations by Cake ('Perhaps, Perhaps, Perhaps'), Reel Big Fish ('There is Nothing Like a Dame') and Moodswings and Neneh Cherry ('Bali Ha'I'). There is the hollow, plaintive 'Dog's Life' by eels which works perfectly with the outback, and a Boy George song 'Welcome to your Life (Woop, Woop)' which is not one of his memorable efforts. Guy Gross composed the instrumental music, and it is adequate. Elliott threw out the first score which was composed by Stewart Copeland, one-third of The Police; this was the score used in the version of the film shown in Cannes.

US mag Billboard observed that the soundtrack, "is a rarity because it stands on its own merits while deftly reflecting the quirky mood of the movie".[79] Few directors have an ear for music to match Elliott's. Angie and Teddy bond over an hysterically off-key rendition of 'There is Nothing Like a Dame' which goes so well that Angie gets the Yank to pull over, then drags him into the back of the Kombi. Teddy's first visit to the pet food factory is overlayed with the exquisitely inappropriate 'Happy Talk', and when Midget's corpse is turned into dog meat it is done to the tune of 'Chop Suey'. The juxtaposition of show tunes and outback harshness is like an aural version of Priscilla's fabrics streaming above the desert floor – the same idea of textural contrast.

The most memorable parts of the soundtrack are the durable songs of 'Rogerson': Rodgers and Hammerstein. Their hits are hummed by Woopites, massacred by Angie, played over the Woop Woop airwaves by Reggie, sung along with at the outdoor cinema and riffed on with enormous wit. Two climactic moments are handed over to the two biggest songs, remixed and put in platform dancing shoes. 'You'll Never Walk Alone' is vivified by Robin S, in a version that is still played at Liverpool FC home games. 'Climb Every Mountain' is torn away from the convent with the Mother Abbess's vocals introduced to the hyperactive beatmaking of Junior Vasquez.

"I wanted Rodgers and Hammerstein music from the get go and we waged a long war to get the rights," Elliott said. "The estate had never once agreed to give any R&H music for anything. Ever. In fact, they're better known for suing everybody who tried. And what's more, they'd never given anything away – as in, for free. Knowing we had a $2 music budget, we went on a crusade. I guess we were lucky because post-*Priscilla* there were a few gay guys in the company there who were fans. So thanks to the old pink bus, I pulled off a coup. We were given access to the whole R&H music library, on a small, low budget Aussie movie, for basically nothing. No other production in history had pulled a deal like this off and I'm still very proud of the fact. But there was a big stumble when Sam [Goldwyn Jnr.] and co. didn't get the R&H angle. They were scared of back-to-back 'old peoples' music. We struck a compromise where we would only use R&H original licensed tracks once the plot had reached Woop Woop. And whether I like it or not, this compromise does serve the film well.

"When R&H takes over, it really takes over. My crème de la crème was the big dance mix of 'Climb Every Mountain'. The R&H estate gave us a flat out 'No!', as this anthem was holy ground. My personality being what it is, I can't take no for an answer. I kept calling, bought flowers, and I camped outside until they were probably feeling a bit sorry for me. The execs told me there was an 11 a.m. board meeting in a few days and Mary Rodgers (Richard Rodgers' wife, who was still alive) would attend and they would ask her permission, but expect bad news.

"I flew to the US and turned up at the office building at 11 a.m. on the day of the board meeting having laid down the remix with Junior Vasquez and barged straight into the boardroom, bypassing a stunned secretary about to call the police. There's Mary Rodgers and I screamed, 'I'm about to be removed by security, I shouldn't be here, but can I just play you this?' And – she loved it. We got immediate approval."

The book

The movie is based on Douglas Kennedy's 1994 novel 'The Dead Heart'. It was a first novel, and reads like it was written by a very young man, although Kennedy was thirty-nine when it was published. The protagonist is an insular American journalist, Nick Hawthorne, who visits Australia on a whim and is ensnared by Angie who drags him back to the town of Wollanup. The prose is functional rather than entrancing, but Kennedy provided the narrative structure used by the film, and many of the imaginative elements of the isolated community and its inhabitants. Daddy (his name in the book; Daddy-O in the movie) and Angie have few if any redeeming features in the novel. The film lets us imagine that, in another place and time, Daddy-O might have led a charge at Gallipoli or fought with honour in the Pacific, but Kennedy sees nothing good in Daddy – or any of the Wollanup locals, with the exception of the too-good-to-be-true Krystal. The other significant difference is that the book is only really interested in Nick (Teddy), whereas in the movie Stephan Elliott shifted the focus so that the Woopites are at least as important as the leading man. Elliott also suggests via several more sympathetic townsfolk that the Woop Woop residents might be reasonable people in a different context, and may even be living a relatively satisfying life on their own terms.

Kennedy's prose reads like a screenplay, but if filmed as written it would not have worked cinematically. Somehow Michael Thomas and Elliott hammered together a script that cleaves close to the plot, setting and character outlines of the novel while also functioning in movie terms. Sometimes this meant changing scenes for the sake of spectacle – for example, in the book Krystal's surfer husband is shot in the back while trying to drive away from town, something revealed to Nick as a secret, whereas in the film Midget is shot halfway up a cliff and the action occurs in real time rather than flashback. In the book's final fight Krystal is shot dead as she leaps between Daddy's gun and Nick. The film gives us a less predictable – albeit silly – climax in the shape of the big red kangaroo. Angie in the book is a gargantuan brute who routinely pins Nick down with physical strength and damages him with her fists, and it is hard to imagine how Nick was ever remotely attracted to her, whereas Susie Porter gave Angie spark and spunk to go with her headstrong egoism. Most crucially, however, Elliott and Thomas introduced great vernacular dialogue and tweaked the characters so that some at least became ne'er-do-wells rather than sociopaths.

Kennedy succeeds in capturing some of the malevolence and darkness extant in the outback. "I needed the security of a town," the novel's narrator observes. "A place where there was plenty of visceral distraction, where you weren't turned in on yourself by all that wide open space. That was the real danger of the Outback: the way its emptiness heightened your creeping self-doubt... it amplifies every little fear, every little tendency towards self-loathing."[80] The screenplay is relatively faithful to the novel, except where it improved it and made it cinematic – but Kennedy was apparently aggrieved at the ways in which his book was perverted as it became a film. He wrote in *The Guardian* that, "selling your novel to a producer is somewhat akin to selling your baby to the first band of highwaymen who have trotted down the road, tempting you with a reasonable purse. From that point on, you have essentially abnegated all moral authority over how said baby will be raised in the future."[81]

There is an alternative, of course. Don't sell your novel. Don't take the production company's dollars.

Remain virginal, pure and in complete control.

It is not impossible for an author to understand the compromise, and that the transaction of selling rights means having to let go. Lloyd Jones, one of the finest English-language novelists alive, visited the set to see his 'Mr Pip' transformed from page to screen. "The question inevitably arises: is the film as good as the book?" he later wrote with good sense and grace. "As meaningless a question would be to ask if the fish was as good as the lamb eaten the previous night?...The best and only approach for a filmmaker adapting a novel is to make the story over...In film, the magic tends to be woven on the surface. The viewer is treated to another's dream. In literature, the reader does the dreaming."[82]

Screenwriter Michael Thomas said via email, "The book's joke-free crap tourism starring the author as a burnt-out journalist – errrggkk! – but the IDEA, this ocker *Brigadoon*, had a lot of promise. First draft I called *Fuck Me Dead*, but guess what, then it was *Bloodnut*, same thing. It was plain sailing, Steph was the first helmer we approached, we met up in LA and there wasn't much I had to give up in pre-prod, primarily Steph's mad idea about bird smuggling. I got rid of the existential malaise and made Teddy a hustler in NYC selling video games out of the back of a truck with a lot of bad debts closing in on his ass, before Steph came up with his bird stuff. Why? Because I'm not gonna go and see a movie about a sadsack journalist. The big idea was the forty-four-foot kangaroo."

Elliott said that, "The writing process was a joy. Michael Thomas is this weird ex-Rolling Stone journo and a hoot to work with. His first draft was full of doofus rock and roll references; Teddy was just a walking jukebox. I then came in with Rodgers and Hammerstein which challenged everything Michael had penned. Michael planted the concept in my head that Woop Woop is a metaphor for Australia. It's too far away. It's Australia within Australia; too far to come to, too far to go. And I ran with this idea as far as I could.

"Michael wrote Susie's character Angie as a beautiful six-foot tall Amazonian goddess. I completely disagreed. A girl from Woop Woop would not look like a fucking supermodel. I fought long and hard on that front. But the thing I love most about Michael (which is why we still have this terrific relationship to this day) is that it's his script, he wrote it, but gave me carte blanche to fuck with it. I have nothing but respect for any writer who can swallow that pill."

Elliott described the infamous dialogue and catch-phrases as, "a mixed bag that somehow works; a collection of old time corkers sprinkled with Michael and my originals. 'Pork sword' comes care of Barry Humphries. 'Beef curtains' is an original of mine which has since become school gym lexicon. Even John Waters has stolen my beef curtains. 'Spam castanets' was another one of mine. I'd throw curve balls like that at Michael and he'd go with it when most other writers would try to shut you down. We were hunting for a catchphrase for Daddy-O, and weren't winning. I'd come up with a handful, as had Michael who was set on 'Fuck me dead', then suddenly Rod opened his mouth and out falls, 'Fahfangoolah'. Entirely his. Perfect."

"We had a lot of fun," Thomas agreed. "Acid test: Stephan is still a mate of mine. For a long time after Cannes the sadsack who wrote the book dined out on the trauma, he ABSOLVED himself in pieces he wrote, like he was Beethoven or something. All he should say is: thanks. We put this loser on the map."

Unconnected further thoughts

Alan Finney is a legendary figure in Australian cinema, as a producer, distributor, actor, writer and Chair of the Australian Film Institute. As well as off-camera involvement in *Welcome to Woop Woop*, he also played the role of Barman. "*Welcome to Woop Woop* is one of my favourite films, and it was a shame that it was so negatively received," Finney said. "I had been involved in the Australian distribution of *Priscilla*, became friends with Stephan Elliot, and regarded him as a really talented film-maker who I wanted to work with again. *Welcome to Woop Woop* was a chance to do this. It was a script I really liked and thought daring, funny and only a film a true Aussie could and would make. I also thought the use of Rodgers & Hammerstein music was fantastic. I was both surprised and disappointed by the critical response. They just didn't get it. Following *Priscilla* and *Muriel's Wedding* I had thought that local commentators would be much more appreciative of the dark humour of the film and its celebration of 'taking the mickey' out of our Australian culture and character."

When Stephan Elliott was twenty-one he landed a gig on his first feature, as Third AD on *The Coca-Cola Kid*. The director was the famed Dusan Makavejev, and it is worth pondering what Elliott absorbed in the experience. The lead character in that film was an American with great hair, Eric Roberts, who always looks out of synch with Australia. (Roberts' unique vocal style makes him seem out of synch with anywhere at all.) He visits a rural enclave ruled by a local strongman, albeit in this case a benign dictator, outside of time and beyond the prevailing culture. These are the obvious links to *Welcome to Woop Woop*. More subtly, there are directorial decisions that are unapologetic and memorable. For example, Makavejev chooses to punctuate a scene of domestic violence with a shot of a cockatoo's cloaca as it expels shit. He chooses to show Greta Scacchi's Terri and her on-screen daughter Rebecca Smart (aged nine at the time of release) naked together in a shower, an option sure to fuel audience uncertainty if not anger. At other times he draws explicit attention to Terri's oral tendencies with lingering scenes of her pulling sticky Turkish delight out of her mouth, putting the edge of her notebook between her lips, sucking on a teaspoon of yoghurt. Perhaps this helped inspire the shots of Angie wrapping her lips around a Cherry Ripe. Even if the influence was not so direct, watching Makavejev work must have encouraged Elliott's fearlessness.

Welcome to Woop Woop is sometimes lumped under the banner of 'Ozploitation'. Filmmaker/researcher Mark Hartley has done sterling work documenting (and celebrating) this underappreciated stream of Australian cinema. His *Not Quite Hollywood: The Wild, Untold Story of Ozploitation!* is a relucent overview of B-movies and genre cinema of the 1970s and early 1980s. The documentary is enormously enjoyable, but also illustrates the differences in intention between those movies and Stephan Elliott's, showing why *Welcome to Woop Woop* is not in fact an Ozploitation flick. The key similarity is the palpable desire to push the boundaries of taste and decorum. Elliott, however, aspires to create something that lasts, that is not purely disposable – not that disposability is necessarily a cinematic sin.

Cineastes routinely deceive themselves by pretending that any given film can be considered as an artistic unity – that this really was supposed to mean that, and that any given choice has been made for the purposes of the movie itself. French thinker Alain Badiou called cinema "an impure art",[83] and indeed it is. The truth of almost all commercially-released films is that they represent the final outcome of a series of compromises, large and small. This decision was taken because the money had run out. That decision was taken because the licence could not be gained for the hit song that was supposed to pin the whole scene together. This decision was made because the lead actor had to leave the shoot after only five days because he was committed to a much larger project that had its schedule brought forward unexpectedly. That decision was taken because shooting at any time other than dawn would have meant coping with eye-piercing reflections from the nearby mobile phone towers. This decision was taken because the name actor kept insisting on changes to her role, and this was the smallest change the director thought she could get away with while still making the actor think she was getting things her way. And so on. And so on.

We know this to be true, but it seems terribly hard to remember. Like children, we prefer to pretend that each movie has arrived into the world fully-formed within a hermetic bubble. Lillian Ross's remarkable 1952 book 'Picture' about the traducing of John Huston's vision over the course of making *The Red Badge of Courage* pinpointed a situation that prevailed prior to that time, and still does today: in the movies, money trumps art every time, and that can be depressing.

Elliott said that the deliberately misheard line from *The Sound of Music* – 'What is it you can't face?' – was laughed at within his family dating back to when he was a child. "A lot of other families got it as well I think, but it never went public till *Woop Woop*," he said. "Now it's a movie musical classic, the catch phrase for Sing-A-Long Sound of Music. I'll never forget Julie Andrews when she saw it. It had been an in-house joke for her and Blake Edwards for years. The gag was finally out of the bag."

Welcome to Woop Woop was produced at the same time as *Oscar and Lucinda*. The bastards of the bush, versus Cate and Ralph and Art. Where do you think cultured people placed their allegiance? In *Oscar and Lucinda* the music is by Beethoven and Bruckner and Bach; the tone is thin-lipped and serious; the obligatory glimpse of Tasmanian Aborigines ends in approved fashion (the whites shoot at them); and so it goes. There is one piece of ambitious image-making in that film, the procession of horses, carriages and the glass church calling to mind the insane procession in Herzog's *Aguirre: The Wrath of God*, but overall it was another unhappy example of the difficulty in transferring Peter Carey's novels to the screen. Of course, there was a much more interesting take on Australia released around that time, but the luvvies didn't care much for it. Elliott recalls that someone on the *Woop Woop* crew pinched twenty t-shirts from the set of the higher-brow film and had them modified: certain members of the Woop Woop family proudly wore shirts saying 'Oscar & Lucinda *Go To The Tip*'.

Scriptwriter Michael Thomas, who writes with the pace and cut-through of a helicopter rotor blade, presaged the approach he took with the screenplay in a punchy piece called 'The decline and fall of Okker chic' written a decade earlier. Firstly he located Paul Hogan's appeal in America not just in his look but in his sound.

Hogan, Thomas wrote, had, "the born-innocent Bondiblue eyes and the straw hair and the seamless amber tan and the sloppy grin and the cauliflower knees you get from kneeling on a surfboard and the whole who-gives-a-root-she's-apples Rogue Okker insouciance he was born with. But it's the verbal they love in L.A. That wacky dinky-di slang. And the vowels – those excruciating A's and E's and oi's ricocheting off the adenoids and resonating up there in the sinuses like a blowfly caught in a bottle of Chiteau Tanunda."[84]

That was 1987, the time of Jenny Kee and Hawkey and Ken Done and gearing up for the masturbation-of-a-nation Bicentenary. Still years away from the how-Aussie-is-that movie boom that produced *Muriel's Wedding* and *Strictly Ballroom* and *The Castle* and *Bootmen*, Thomas had the acuteness of vision to see where things were going – and the clear-sightedness to realise that the Australia about to be celebrated and satirised was already gone: "Stone the crows! It was amazing. Suddenly all this Okker junk had meaning. Cling peaches! Jaffas! Minties! Lamingtons! Hoadley's Violet Crumble Bars! Pelaco shirts! Akubra hats! These things had become cultural artifacts, as though Australia had not just a look, not just weather, not just good oysters and cold beer and big surf and funny accents, not just infinite space and light and waterfrontage but a culture. If you like ironies this is it: As Okker Chic sweeps the civilized world and all an Australian has to do is open his mouth and eyes light up all around the room, here's a memo to all you Paul Hogan fans – you missed it. Tough luck. It's all a dream. It's not there anymore..."[85]

The chutzpah and crazy-bravery required to create a parallel reality – really, an alternative universe – cannot be overestimated. Dr Johnson said that with writing, a seed is no easier to create than an oak tree.

Similarly, a cogent and complete township like Woop Woop is no easier to make work than a separate planet in a sci-fi blockbuster.

Actor Anne Baxter remembers speaking with Patrick White: "I haltingly tried to voice some of my vague apprehensions about the hostile presence of the Australian bush. Patrick looked down at me, his eyes the same opalescent augers that first dismayed me, and spoke in his peculiar, faintly acrid voice. 'But don't you know? Australia doesn't like people.'"[86] The Nobel Laureate might have understood and appreciated the gothic grotesquery of Woop Woop. The fevered interrelationships within the sealed world of that isolated hamlet may well have appealed to his singular sense of humour. At the very least, the portrayal of the desert landscape rejecting its European inhabitants like a wound expelling an infected splinter would have elicited a thin-lipped grin – had he not died in 1990.

Getting Barry Humphries was a coup, but not a complete surprise. For a performer of genius, he has appeared in a lot of movies that are best forgotten: *It's Not the Size That Counts*, *Shock Treatment*, *The Marsupials: The Howling III* and *Pterodactyl Woman from Beverly Hills*, among others. (Intriguingly, Elliott has said that his first choice for the role of Blind Wally was former Prime Minister Bob Hawke.) Elliott and Humphries was a potent combination. The feted performer could have been used to many ends, but the director chose to have him hunched like a buzzard, in grubby overalls, with tape and cardboard over his spectacles, and brought out the misanthropy beneath the surface.

(Max Cullen thought Humphries' turn was

derivative, an interesting and not completely improbable theory. The veteran actor wrote in his memoir that Humphries took him and some confreres to the Garrick Club in London. Cullen watched him closely during dinner, and, "he obviously watched me closely as well because when the movie *Welcome to Woop Woop* came out later with him playing a blind motor mechanic, service station attendant, he sent up gutless the character I created in cult movie *Runnin' on Empty*. Now I can say I've been played by Dame Edna!"[87])

Being Stephan Elliott

As a director, Elliott is routinely pigeonholed as 'flamboyant' or 'outrageous', given credit for his clever use of music and good eye and not much else. However, Antonia Barnard identified that, "Stephan is a director with an extensive knowledge of film and its history. In the structure of his films there always appears to be classical references to cinematic masterpieces, often not acknowledged." Finola Dwyer also pointed to his underrated skills as an actors' director: "Steph is a director with a great vision and a strong sense of how he sees the film. He is also a performance driven director as well as being incredibly visual. He doesn't sacrifice performance for style."[88] Susie Porter described him as, "an amazing director. He was outrageous, nothing was too much, and you could add things and he would happily go with it. He has an amazing energy. And he's smart. There is no-one like Stephan Elliott. No-one in the world. He's a true original."

"People have different approaches to directing," Elliott said. "There are tyrants who need to have control of every element. Others surround themselves with good crew who tell them how to direct. My approach is to give everybody boundaries. When I have 500 or 600 moving parts, I view my job as herding them all in the same direction. Sometimes you have to rein them in, while trying to give them space to move in the right direction within the boundaries. When something's really wrong, you have to put your foot down. Which happens.

"Then there's the cinematic Chinese whispers. Everybody hears/sees things differently in the long chain of film making. I love collaboration. Writing can get very lonely. Making the film is the social/collaborative part. My creative team gets carte blanche. They know I trust them, and usually they can do whatever they want. Even the actors, which has surprised me these last few years. The key is to make sure you've employed really good actors. *Easy Virtue* had no rehearsal time because the cast were all filming other projects simultaneously. I couldn't get them all in the same room at once. That became a lesson in collaboration. We'd get to the floor each day with nothing but each other to trust, and wing it.

"In the last week of that shoot I was completely backed into a corner, twenty shots planned with two minutes left to do them all – this after no rehearsal. I'm banging my head on the table yelling, 'I can't work in this way' and KST [Kristin Scott Thomas] barks, 'What are you talking about? This is the most fun I've had in years. Don't overthink it. Let's just go.' We got it in, an incredibly complex indoor/outdoor night shot in two takes, basically because I just let the actors drive."

Elliott has spent two-thirds of his life in the film industry, giving him a long perspective on the craft and his own position in movie land. This is enhanced by a worldview forged in part by a near-death experience, and the long haul of recovery.

"I'm told constantly that I could have had a big career," Elliott said. "I could have been Baz Luhrmann or whatever, but I didn't allow it to happen. My first feature *Frauds* completely fucked me up the arse. Locked out of my cutting room, removed from my first film, an experience in the most brutal Hollywood behaviour imaginable. I was taken over, and at twenty-six years old the bastards absolutely broke me. I was so damaged I vowed never to go through it again.

"That first experience has been a gift of sorts. I am now completely aware there are people in this business who make it their business to completely destroy you. I may not have had the American career, but that's by choice. I don't trust them. I've been told so many lies by so many cheats and arseholes. The amount of times I've had food spat in my face, being told that I 'will never work in this town again'. Now I love this kinda talk. It's great sport.

"After *Frauds*, *Priscilla* producer Al Clark did a brilliant job, protecting and boosting to get my confidence back up again. *Woop Woop* was a reaction against what I went through with *Frauds*. It was a complete 'Fuck you'. There's a lot of anger in the film, a lot of resentment, and it was very cathartic, but the film got taken off me again as punishment. I did go way too far with the original cut as I was so determined to push the envelope. Then I got the bill."

On 11 September 2001 Elliott was in New York. He arranged to meet a female actor near the World Trade Centre to discuss a project he was developing based on an Ayn Rand novel. Five minutes after the scheduled meeting time, the first plane hit. "It took me a couple of years of therapy to get through that one. Really fucked with my head. It was another good wake-up call in a weird way."

The other big 'wake-up call' came in 2004 when he almost died after skiing off a cliff in the French Alps. With classic Elliott brio he told a journalist, "I hit a rock, cock-first, so the damage down there is extraordinary. Lost my spleen, ruptured my bladder, shattered my pelvis. I have to carry a catheter around these days because the waterworks freeze up sometimes. You have to ram the tip down the old fella."[89]

As he lay on the mountainside with a collection of broken bones and haemorrhaging internally, he was tended to by a group of young French ski instructors. Elliott, still conscious and believing his spine was damaged, told them not to move him. They made the point that if they left him to wait for the paramedics he would die. He was hoisted in a fibreglass 'banana boat' and loaded onto a fire truck. It rushed him to meet an oncoming ambulance for an emergency transfusion. "By that time it was really bad," Elliott said. "I mean, I was in shitloads of agony. Finally the ambulance arrived, the nurse jumped out, opened the kit and it was empty: she'd grabbed the wrong one. No blood. I was watching it all, they were all screaming at each other and I turned to the doctor and said, 'How long have I got if I don't get any blood?' He said, 'About 20 minutes.'"[90]

While his life was in the balance, Elliott was also told that his injuries meant he may not walk again. "That's a very weird moment to go through: to be told, 'This is it.' So I went out with this stupid grin on my face, and then suddenly woke up a day-and-a-half later. The first thing I said when I came to is, 'What the fuck am I doing here?' And so began two years of absolute hell! (laughs)"[91]

There are gruesome photos of Elliott lying in a hospital bed with an array of titanium pins piercing his flesh and screwed into his bones, an exoskeleton devised to support his smashed interior. He broke his back, pelvis and legs but not, as the durable cliché goes, his spirit. "There's very little I'm scared of anymore," he said. "I've had my moment, I went through the fear factor, I know what it's like to have (death) waved in front of you. But what I did realise was, it's really not that frightening."[92]

Counterintuitively, the accident gave him the mental and emotional fortitude to re-enter the world of film. "After you've lived and walked through a scenario like that, what else can hurt? I breezed into *Easy Virtue*. They screwed me financially of course, but they always will. Whenever I'm cornered nowadays I think back to that dialogue in the hospital. Nothing can come close after that. Healthwise, my body's fine at the moment; my brain's still fourteen years old. I'm okay with that."

Elliott says he has always felt like an outsider – at Sydney Grammar; in a film industry that did not value his idiosyncratic talent, let alone his precocity; as an artist within mainstream Australia; and within the sometimes narrow parameters of the gay community – and that all of his films have been outsider tales. This is an advantage;

often the best position from which to appraise a situation is on the outside. "I have spent years of my life outback," Elliott said. "From about eighteen to twenty-six I was an AD, and many of the films I was on were shot deep desert. I'm still thrilled to get out there, but I know how racist, dangerous and homophobic it can get.

"The location recces for *Priscilla* were probably the building blocks for *Woop Woop*. Brian Breheny the cinematographer, Al Clark the producer and myself went deep outback exploring. I was, believe it or not, still in the closet – I only formally came out publicly in 2012 – so *Priscilla* was me, a long slow coming out movie. I'm not going to lie, I was a good-looking twenty-five-year-old kid wandering around the desert dressed like a poof, and nearly had the shit beaten out of me about ten times. 'Where are you from, Uranus?'

"There's an entire *Woop Woop* sub-plot which was cut out involving Paul Mercurio, Midget the hairdresser, married to Dee Smart's character Krystal. There's a scene where Teddy goes to visit Krystal and Daddy-O comes in late at night pissed and it's really creepy. You don't know if he's going to hug her, hit her or rape her. Teddy has to hide under the bed where he finds fifty gay magazines. The gag is Krystal married a gay guy and brought him back to Woop Woop, so the secret is that she's still a virgin. Daddy-O knew Midget was a poof, the perfect excuse to shoot him. So there's me still coming out again. God I'd love to put that moment back in.

"Another reason *Woop Woop* bombed: timing," he said, echoing Porter. "Australians had just discovered the internet, BMWs and frappuccinos, all gearing up for the new millennium with new lives trying to leave their cultural cringe behind. And most of those people have never been more than fifty kilometres from the coast. Deep out back had not changed that much: still nasty, tough as brass. So what I couldn't put into *Priscilla*, I saved for *Woop Woop*. And Australians didn't like seeing it anymore. It was time for them all to move on.

"We don't know who we are any more, but we are not alone. It's happening right around the world. Globalisation is destroying cultures left, right and centre. The metaphor in *Woop Woop* about Australia being so far away – it's gone now, thanks to technology. It's killed the outback. When I was making movies deep desert as a teenager even the Motorola radios wouldn't get you 100 metres, so we were reduced to flashing the headlights on the catering truck or making hand signals. At night you'd sit in the bar and talk to people. You go out there now, everyone's on their tablets, androids and iPhones. The isolation that created those communities has evaporated.

"We're in such trouble at the moment in Australia. We have completely lost our national identity. We don't know who we are. I was at a writer's conference last year and everyone was trying to work out the secret formula to a great Australian film. I stood up and asked, 'What's an Australian? You don't know who you are any more.' We've moved past shrimps and Holdens, we're not allowed to do anything politically incorrect. Can't be too loud, can't be too colourful. Can't be too dark. Who'd have suspected that two of the most successful films of the last few years would have been *Samson and Delilah* and *The Sapphires*? Incredibly successful films in Australia. No play at all internationally. And that really tells you something.

"I feel for youngsters who ask, 'How do we make a successful Australian film?' Truth is, the world is honestly not interested in Australia any more. We were flavour of the month for a decade or so, but the product we churn out now has joined the global mush. Even going in to *Woop Woop* I thought, this is the last time anyone is ever going to try to get away with this. I knew that there were a lot of Melbourne and Sydneyites who would be outraged by it, and I was right. But what have we replaced it with? We are no longer interesting or distinctive, but no-one really cares or understands that old Australia any more, and every day that goes past they get less interested."

But not Elliott. He is still interested, despite spending a lot of his adult life based far from Australian shores. "I still fucking love it," he said. "I occasionally meet folks, older Australians, who have those old Aussie characteristics and I think: please don't die. You're gold."

Fitting *Welcome to Woop Woop* within the Elliott oeuvre

Frauds

Elliott's first feature is a strange confection. A demented insurance investigator, Richard Copping (Phil Collins) decides to make life a misery for a couple who have committed insurance fraud. The mood is dark; the sets are gaudy. The theme is games of chance. The set design of the interior of Copping's place is maximalist and lurid, matching the character's insanity. It is a completely different aesthetic to Woop Woop but shows the same enthusiasm for creating a memorable, somewhat surreal built environment. Another link to his later film comes when he wants to show that Copping is bad as well as mad. Elliott achieves this by having the investigator sacrifice a box of fluffy white bunnies to some large canines for his sadistic amusement. Similarly, the depth of Daddy-O's depravity was signalled by the slaughter of Teddy's dog.

Producer Al Clark said that *Frauds* was "one of the most confident first films I have seen, and one of the most original."[93] It certainly showcased what Elliott could do, and provides an introduction to some of his preferred camera tricks and techniques, including the hard zoom into character's faces, plunging vertical shots, and shooting mirrors and other reflective surfaces. 'I've Got You Under My Skin' is used as a theme for Copping, a good Elliott song choice, but the orchestral score is over-insistent. Collins is excellent and remains consistent throughout a movie that feels like it was edited by committee. It was deft casting, subverting Collins' unthreatening teddy-bear persona, and Elliott elicited the musician/actor's best effort on film. This is part of Elliott's skill, pulling showreel-worthy performances from stars – including Terence Stamp, Rod Taylor, Jessica Biel and even Olivia Newton-John.

The director said that *Frauds* was the first 'baby' taken away from him. "I was physically kicked out of the cutting room which was, in turn relocated from Sydney to LA," he said. "My whole post crew was also fired and a new editor was brought in. I was not even allowed to see what they were doing. That's fired."

The Adventures of Priscilla, Queen of the Desert

Considered Elliott's signature piece, *Priscilla* was an uproariously successful bagatelle that hit the world's screens at the right time. The film was always destined for wild enthusiasm from a niche audience (drag show enthusiasts), but to the considerable financial pleasure of the producers it was a monster mainstream hit as well.

Elliott directed *Priscilla* like the Richard Copping (see *Frauds*) of filmmaking, as if the governing criteria was whether or not he was being amused. This led to missteps. The Filipina caricature, Cynthia, is an example of something that probably seemed funny at the time but sits awkwardly. Tom O'Regan claimed that Cynthia, "perpetuates stereotypes which lead to excessive violence."[94] Producer Al Clark countered that, "The film is a gentle satire with enormous affection for its characters"[95] and that Cynthia is a misfit like the other lead characters.

In a completely different way, the encounter with the desert Aboriginal people that results in cross-cultural sharing, many toothy smiles and good will to all is an exercise in stereotyping. The caricature here is one that seems to exist only in Australian films, not in our regular national life, and that is the idea of the beaming blackfella, the good-hearted Indigene who is always more sophisticated than the white characters suspect, but forgiving and compliant at the same time. Little was sacred in *Priscilla*, but it still tiptoed away from presenting credible Aboriginal characters.

Philip Brophy argued that the scene in which the drag queens walk the streets of Broken Hill, "is unfounded, fatuous and desultory, sharply drawing attention to its horrid mimicry."[96] The whole Broken Hill stint is problematic. In a dodgy pub scene, Bernadette conquers transphobia – with bitchy misogyny. It is hard to see this as much of a triumph. Denounced by an unattractive bigot called Shirley, Bernadette delivers the clunky slapdown: "Now listen here, you mullet. Why don't you just light your tampon, and blow your box apart? Because it's the only bang you're ever gonna get, sweetheart!" And huzzah, the pub is on the side of the drag performers. Shirley is just a woman, and old and ugly to boot. Take that.

One of the myths we tell ourselves as Australians is that we are upfront people – a furphy. On the contrary, we tend to keep our disapproval quiet, or mutter about it out of the sides of our mouths. We might bash poofters, but the most vicious verbal attacks on those we dislike are more likely to occur in absentia. The scene where a drug-addled Felicia is chased by outraged Coober Pedy blokes rings hollow because the homo-hate speech delivered by Frank is too windy. The punch to Felicia's jaw makes sense; that is the most articulate form of communication for a Neanderthal. Having Bernadette arrive like an avenging angel to drop the bully with a groin shot causing the dozen angry rednecks to turn and run away is a silly fantasy. They may not have stayed around for a debate on cismale attitudes towards The Other, but they would not have fled from a fight with three drag queens, one of whom was already on the ground – with or without the assistance of butch Bill Hunter. Brophy thinks that it is a misguided attempt to win acceptance for the outcast trio; that by punching on we learn that, "these ugly poofters are true blue Aussies after all."[97]

The motive power of the film is the encounter between diametric opposites – the drag queens as the apotheosis of inner-city liberality smashing up against the outback as the home of regressive, repressive redneck Australia. As Bernadette says, "I don't know if that ugly wall of suburbia's been put there to stop them getting in, or us getting out." The heart-warming take-home-from-the-cinema moment is when a representative of one side of that wall (Terence Stamp's Bernadette) and a representative of the other side (Hunter's Bob) fall in love. However, in a film where everything goes, where vaginal bazookaing is no problemo, Bernadette and Bob's relationship is ridiculously coy. There is not even a kiss, let alone a sex scene.

A fundamental problem is that the three central characters seem to be playing at camp, not embodying it, although Stamp (who looks uncomfortably like the ageing Madonna Ciccone) is impressive. Was there a fear that the mainstream audience would not have coped with real live gay men playing gay men? Guy Pearce puts everything into his over the top characterisation, but the safety net is that he is obviously 'acting'. When Hugo Weaving, a transvestite with a wife and child who apparently prefers sex with men, agonises over what his sexual identity might be, how reassuring it is for the predominantly heterosexual mainstream audience to know that good ol' Hugo is just pretending on our behalf.

In many ways the film feels forced, a confection built up around the central imagery that Elliott wanted to capture. The plethora of jokes that he picked up in barrooms and drag performances and wherever else are shoehorned together to create the dialogue. Some of the jokes are great; others function as gags but not as dialogue, and fall from the actors' mouths like housebricks. Additionally, within the parameters of the situation he has drawn, the plot is predictable and the character arcs are truncated and uninvolving.

If this is an overly harsh critique, it is deliberately so – intended as a corrective to the perception that *Priscilla* is a masterwork and, by extension, that it was a dizzying zenith followed by the miserable nadir of *Welcome to Woop Woop*. The latter film is more consistent, more interesting, and more genuinely transgressive because it does not try to make out that everything is sunny and there is a happy future in store for every character.

For all this, there are enjoyable elements in *Priscilla*. Elliott demonstrated yet again that he has the rare gift of a stunning eye and a brilliant ear. There are two pivotal images in the film. The first (which is given two equally gorgeous incarnations) is the long shot of an expanse of billowing fabric streaming from a drag artiste in a giant stiletto on top of a bus roaring through the desert while opera blares. Has there ever been a better visual idea in an Australian film? The second pivotal image is three drag queens in full regalia at the crest of King's Canyon – Elliott's enactment of his line, "It's just what this country needs: a cock in a frock on a rock."

Polarisers were used to achieve very blue skies, and colour enhancer brought out the beauty of the landscape, making it look intricate rather than lumpen. The energy in the film is innate, generated by ideas and Elliott's sense of humour rather than plot. Even Brophy felt it exemplified, "a unique brand of nihilistic glory in which white Australia excels."[98] Producer Clark praised, correctly, its "total absence of ingratiation"[99]. The movie exists on its own terms with little resonance beyond that, but the director maintains his usual shoulder-shrugging stance: "It is what it is," Elliott said. "And it's still making friends."

Eye of the Beholder

The cast is strong, the cinematography is typically clever, but the plot is labyrinthine and turns on the main character, Eye (Ewan McGregor), making highly implausible decisions. It is still recognisable as an Elliott film, just, but there are only a few small consolations for the dogged viewer. For example, early on the camera takes us behind a service station, where for no apparent reason there is a huge pile of discarded cash registers. Random and intriguing. Eye's fixation on his dead daughter reaches a creepy apotheosis in a disturbing scene inside his apartment where four or five ghosts of his daughter sing and clatter simultaneously. It is a great representation of grief-induced madness and difficult to watch. When a railway cleaner discovers a corpse in a train toilet the revelation comes via an extravagant expulsion of water. There is an ongoing conceit regarding snow domes, and Elliott plays with this visually, resolving a cityscape into the interior of a snow dome on several occasions. In a dank watering hole there is a monkey walking along the bar; who knows why. A revolving worm's-eye shot of the inside of a circular staircase resolves into a stylised eye. There are dolly and crane shots of bewildering complexity, and his trademark rack focusing, pulling attention from one figure to another in two-shots.

Beyond those moments of interest, it is a mess. The narrative lacks momentum because it is hard to feel close to McGregor's closed-down character, and when the plot's coherence dips away we do not care enough to try to work it all out. The godforsaken Nevada hamlet of Techatticup where the film's main turning point occurs is presented from a distance, looking down at the scant buildings inside a ring of mountains – a small American idea of Woop Woop – but well before the denouement the director and the audience is defeated.

"*Eye of the Beholder* was a shitfight from the word

go," Elliott said. "It was a difficult script, an unbelievably complex piece of work, outside my genre, playing in a sandpit not natural to me. I got into bed with legitimate criminals masquerading as producers, and they screwed me from every possible angle. The film made a lot of money, and I lost everything. I sank my heart, soul and bank balance into it, then suddenly everyone abandoned ship and I was left to complete the film on my own. By the end I was writing, producing, directing and financing it myself to get it finished. I put my life on the line to finish that fucker, then the LA 'producers' went under and I lost the lot. Any profits from the film went into the bankruptcy pool of (executive producer) Mark Damon, who opened a new company about two weeks later guilt free. *Eye* made a shitload of money. Theatrically it was number one at the US box office for two weeks [but quickly fell from the spot]. It was one of the highest grossing DVDs of that year, back-end sales were phenomenal – and I never saw a cent. Even my fee."

Easy Virtue

This is an English period piece without the pompous ponderousness of Merchant Ivory. Elliott and Sheridan Jobbins wrote the screenplay from Noel Coward's play. The decision to confine most of the action to a manor house seemed to free Elliott; the narrow parameters of setting allowed him to go deeper, as in *Welcome to Woop Woop*, as distinct from the sprawl of *Priscilla* and *Eye of the Beholder*. The rambling ancestral home is full of odd pieces of taxidermy, framed pictures of dogs, mirrors of every description, and period art. As ever, Elliott studs the film with unusual shots and camera angles, most notably the recurring device of filming a reflected image – with the reflection found in various mirrors, the eye of a telescope, a spoon, a silver salver, sunglasses, a black billiard ball and the lid of a gramophone player. Jessica Biel has never been more glamorous, and Kristin Scott Thomas never more fascinating. The music is fabulous, artfully selected from the priceless catalogues of Coward and Cole Porter, and superbly played.

After the halfway-mark the narrative slows and the pleasures of the movie are mainly to do with style and surface, not story. Elliott could be charged with not selling the plot developments hard enough to retain interest. However, the climactic dance between Biel and Colin Firth is a masterpiece of eroticism and psychological revelation.

"I like *Easy Virtue*," Elliott said. "It's a good movie. It just hit the screens at the wrong time. We had a standing ovation at the premiere screening in Toronto, ripping up the seats, a huge hit on our hands. Eight o'clock the next morning was the 2008 stock market crash. The pre-sales we had lined up around the block disappeared in seconds, everyone went into lockdown, and the film really struggled to find a market. We made a calculated decision to set the ending of *Easy Virtue* on Christmas Eve and now it screens around the world as a Christmas movie. Very good call."

A Few Best Men

This wedding romp links to *Welcome to Woop Woop* in various ways. It begins with Elliott's pet device of a self-contained scene set in the other half of the world (England/New York), a shot of an aeroplane, then plunging the deracinated character/s deep into Australia. He elicits a wonderful bigger-than-I-thought-you-could-be performance from an Australian long resident in America (Olivia Newton-John/Rod Taylor) and follows the fortunes of a pretty but limited leading man (Xavier Samuel/Johnathon Schaech).

The direction is competent rather than inspired, the script is derivative and wholly lacking in surprises, and the ambition is never above middle-brow. In 1998 Elliott told FilmInk, "I make movies to keep myself entertained. I don't mind being quite selfish about this. Once you start getting into the business of giving everybody what they want, you're effectively making American movies." It was a stance he could only maintain for so long.

One of the big scenes of the film, the chaos at a formal party, was done with more spark as long ago as Chaplin's *City Lights*. Another major scene, the hideous best man's speech, is less fun than the equivalent in *Dimboola*. *A Few Best Men* is not a particularly bad movie, but it is completely inessential, and adds nothing to Elliott's list of achievements.

"*A Few Best Men* I did for the money," Elliott said. "Biggest paycheque I've had in my life. I didn't write it. The script had problems, but pay me enough and I'll look the other way. I sat in the director's chair and said 'action', had a laugh, did my job and went home. It was fun to make, but there is virtually nothing of me in that film. It is what it says on the label and it bought me a nice flat in Bondi. I thought it was about time to earn some money."

Killing Priscilla

Not an Elliott film, but an insight-filled doco Lizzy Gardiner made in 1999. While working with Elliott on *Eye of the Beholder* she did double-duty, augmenting her usual gorgeous work on costume design with a directorial role, capturing the behind-camera proceedings. The resultant documentary is a fifty-five minute lesson in why you should not become a filmmaker. The complications, thwarted dreams and humiliations of the film industry are laid bare; it is the documentary equivalent of Lillian Ross's 'Picture'. It shows Elliott's excruciating path through shooting in sub-freezing temperature to meetings with creepy sales executives, a strong-minded film distributor and a general loss of faith in the product as he tries to finish reshooting it himself, with his own money and a shoestring crew.

Gardiner tips us to her feelings about Elliott when she asks Ewan McGregor, "Is it hard to put yourself in the hands of a giant fourteen-year-old?" The adult fourteen-year-old is trying to rebound from the caning that *Welcome to Woop Woop* received. "*Woop Woop* has been a disaster in every sense of the word," Elliott says on camera while doing his laundry in a hotel bath. "I think I'm being punished for that. *Priscilla*'s become a bit of a ball and chain. It went way beyond the success it really should have deserved. I do believe that. It was lots of fun, but Academy Awards, Golden Globes, come on – it's not that good a movie."

Later Elliott refers to the impact of *Welcome to Woop Woop* on his career, saying, "My last film was a flop, it's been considered a flop. I've copped some really bad brownie points for that one and a lot of people are saying, 'You'd better come through with the goods next time or your career's finished'."

This threat to his vocation is exemplified with a great anecdote: "I get a phone call from MGM and Scott Rudin, who is one of the big hotshots at Paramount...

he's got a reputation as one of the ultimate Hollywood bullies, but after *Priscilla* he tried to be my best friend. He rang every now and then, always sent scripts over. MGM rang the other day and said, 'Scott Rudin has asked if he can see *Woop Woop*.' This was before the film opened. Sent a print over to Scott's office, it got sent back three days later. I rang the office to see what Scott thought of it and he wouldn't take my call. I rang about five times over five weeks to find out his opinion of the movie and he wouldn't return my call. Eventually his assistant said, 'Look, I don't think he's ever going to return your call'. I said, 'If Mr Rudin, after all the shit he's been, you know, about being my best friend won't come to a telephone call, then this is the last time we're ever going to have any form of communication ever again.' And his assistant said, 'I think that would be fine with Mr Rudin.'"

Elliott's feelings about the film biz are summed up simply: "If I had money, would I make movies? No."

Reflecting years later, Elliot said, "For a couple of years I couldn't watch *Killing Priscilla*. There is an eight hour cut which is soul destroying. Lizzy did some cool wire taps filming telephone conversations with these executives saying they're going to fuck me, destroy me and kill me. Then on camera next day I'd ask them to their faces if they still wanted to fuck, kill and destroy me. 'No, no, we'd never do that. Let's do lunch.' All smiles and slaps on the back. At the end of the day, we would have been sued, so Lizzy cut them out. The doco was torturous for a couple of years, but now I think it's highly amusing."

Three older cousins of *Welcome to Woop Woop*

Elliott was a multiplex kid, in thrall to Stephen Spielberg's gargantuan big-screen successes. He does not remember watching a lot of Australian movies growing up. Despite this, he is part of a small local industry that has a rich collective unconscious. Whether he intended it or not, Elliott's *Welcome to Woop Woop* linked to a number of Aussie films that predated it.

Wake in Fright

This very fine Australian movie was made by a Canadian, produced by Americans and a Norwegian, shot by a Londoner and starred two Englishmen. Gary Bond, one of the Poms, looked like a refugee from *Blow Up* and his mannered, troubled performance gave the film its centre. The show is stolen by his countryman Donald Pleasance whose alcoholic doctor is quietly terrifying.

On the director commentary to the DVD release, Ted Kotcheff called the film, "a study in the corrosive loneliness of all the characters." When he wants to indicate the way Bond's schoolteacher is divorced from the community, he twins him with the character of an old Aboriginal man on the train. This is a ruthless Australia, with citizens as brutish and unforgiving as the landscape itself. The famous two-up scene featured dozens of actual two-up players in Sydney, which perhaps explains why their faces are so perfect. If they were available a quarter-century later they could have easily been Woopites. The same goes for most citizens of Bundanyabba ('the Yabba').

Kotcheff used a technique beloved by Elliott, with characters listening to music from a jarringly different time, place and context – in this case the ironic playing of glossy, helium-light Italian soprano Amelita Galla-Curci singing 'Caro Nome' from Verdi's 'Rigoletto' in Doc Tydon's shambles of a hovel.

The film became infamous for the kangaroo shooting scene where men go screaming through the bush in a chopped 1959 Ford Fairlaine. The footage used was taken on an expedition with a real kangaroo shooting crew. It makes the pitchforking of dead kangaroos in *Welcome to Woop Woop* look restrained. Kotcheff also placed a big light in Doc Tydon's shack, which is handled as effectively as the huge light on the Woop Woop lookout tower. The director used this light to mimic the spotlight on the roo-shooting car; it shines without pity into the schoolteacher's eyes, then Doc grapples and sexually 'butchers' him like one of the roos.

There was a production decision to exclude all cool colours from the film, with the sole exception of John Grant's flashback memory of his girlfriend in the ocean. Rough Australian bush faces are captured in close-up, the masculine dialogue and physicality drenches every scene in testosterone, and even the women offer little mercy or comfort – including the strange semi-succubus Janette Hynes, played by Kotcheff's wife Sylvia Kay.

Reflecting on the themes of the movie decades later, Kotcheff spoke of the story and the setting, saying, "The emptiness is claustrophobic. It imprisons you." One last *Welcome to Woop Woop* link in a film that has many: a Major Mitchell cockatoo is kept in Tydon's hut.

The Barry McKenzie films

The connections between *Welcome to Woop Woop* and the Bazza films – *The Adventures of Barry McKenzie* and *Barry McKenzie Holds His Own* – include the presence of Barry Humphries and the schemata of a 'fish out of water' as Bazza struggles in the urban jungle of 1970s London. The key connection however is the verve of the vernacular-stuffed dialogue, and the glee with which great Antipodean sayings (extant and invented) are presented.

Australia's first 'R' certificate was pinned onto *Stork* in 1971. Tim Burstall's showcase of Bruce Spence's character (written by David Williamson) has not aged well; to watch it today is to give thanks for feminism and the maturation of the local film industry. However its commercial success and broad approach to sex and language opened the gate for the Barry McKenzie sagas, 70s movies such as *Alvin Purple* and– and, ultimately, *Welcome to Woop Woop*.

The Adventures of Barry McKenzie has many weak points and many joys. Bruce Beresford was still learning how to shape a film but was shrewd enough to provide ample room for the dialogue. He has cameos from Humphries, Peter Cook and Spike Milligan (and, if you look closely, John Clarke). He has Bazza quaffing an aphrodisiac of prawns and curry. He includes a song called 'My One-eyed Trouser Snake'. He gets Gough Whitlam involved. He has Aunt Edna Everage say to Barry, "You're going to break a few hearts tonight. Just let your Auntie whisk off your cradle-cap, and pick out those little custard corners." This is the Elliott too-much-is-never-enough ethos in action.

Shannon Harvey called it, "a horribly dated and theatrically over-the-top exaggeration of our crass sense of humour and our cultural identity," but he also considers the movie, "the very first to hold up a mirror to our uniqueness and utter strangeness"[100].

Barry McKenzie Holds His Own is a less successful

film but it steers closer to the spirit of the original comic strip, so the biggest star in the show is Humphries' writing. Thus we have Bazza saying, "I'm that randy I could root the hair on a barber shop floor," and, "I hope your balls turn to bicycle wheels and backpedal up your arse," and ranting in jail that, "there'd be no Mother England if it wasn't for Australia. Our fighting men came over here when you Poms were ready to throw in the towel. Musso and them slimy yellow nips would've flattened this dump if it hadn't been for me uncles and their superlative fighting spirit. I mean the game was nearly up for youse poms, no risk. And if it hadn't been for Australia, Musso and them slant-eyed pricks would've strung every white kiddie up by the pills and gone chocka-block with all the nurses and bus conductresses."

Humphries kept some of the best/worst lines for himself. When uppity Rhonda Cutforth-Jones asks her, "Have you ever balled another chick, Mrs Everage?," Humphries' Aunt Edna replies, "I may be old fashioned, young woman, but lesbianism has always left a nasty taste in my mouth." And, doing his best for racial harmony, when Bazza says, "I'm that thirsty I could drink out of a Japanese wrestler's jockstrap," Edna makes the immortal riposte, "Oh Barry don't make such crude remarks about our dear little stunted slant-eyed yellow friends."

Whatever the differences in intention and execution, these films are spiritual godless-parents to *Priscilla* and especially *Welcome to Woop Woop*.

The Cars That Ate Paris

Peter Weir's breakthrough 1974 film (known in other places as *The Cars That Eat People*) was a small masterclass in capturing rural Australia on Panavision. It veers closer to the conventions of the horror movie than *Welcome to Woop Woop*, but there are many points of crossover. Where Weir let himself go into the darkness, Elliott explored the depths of weirdness – which is not to say that Weir's work does not get pretty strange. An early signal comes when we see locals shoving a calf into the boot of an old Austin A40. Great image, and no attempt at explanation.

The township of Paris – which we first glimpse by looking downwards in long-shot – is isolated and insular. Things that do not seem normal to outsiders have started to seem normal to the locals. For example, the bizarre dress-ups at the Pioneer Ball which include shepherd costumes and crooks, cardboard hats, fake bears and adapted cereal packets. The local cottage industry is the cannibalising of car wrecks, and the screaming delight of Paris's denizens at car smashes, races and stunts is unnerving. At one point we see Gormon carrying a severed car door like a shield, graffitied with the word 'pig'. We know it is wrong, even if we can't quite say why. An even better example of this comes when Bruce Spence (Charlie) makes a hanging wind chime out of purloined Jaguar hood ornaments, then mimes as if to deep throat one of them, a transgressive aside that defies simple rationality.

The power at the centre of the town, and the film, is John Meillon's Mayor. This is one of his greatest roles, and an interesting counterpoint to Daddy-O. The Mayor tells outsider Arthur Waldo that, "Nobody leaves Paris. No-one!" It is a familiar convention of the horror genre, the hero trapped in an isolated place that no-one can escape. Scott Hocking wrote that, "The insular outback society populated by xenophobic eccentrics (such as in Paris) are as much a subversion of the established notion of rural hospitality as the ugly Australians of the Yabba and Woop Woop,"[101] but of course the Woopites are insular and xenophobic and eccentric as well.

The Cars That Ate Paris is a film of clever visual ideas in which rural angst is married to schlock sensibility. Fire is transformative if not redemptive, as seen when Len's car is torched in the main street as summary justice (or when Daddy-O places Ginger on the Woop Woop funeral pyre). After the flames, people can move on. While the film is not as inventive with language as some others, it does include the Old School War Cry performed by The Mayor which captures intrinsically Australian elements of prideful chauvinism and naïve inventiveness, the spirit of football song and corroboree chant – as well as having a kangaroo or two loose in the top paddock:

> "Woomera, woomera, babaloo, boomerang
> Crocodile, kookaburra, wombat, orang-utan,
> Wee-ho, Wey-ho, Thurramungamine,
> Quandong, billabong, gunner bluey pine,
> Platypus, emu, wallaby, roo,
> Ibis, brolga, the white cockatoo,
> Nurra burra, carrah, coolamon, bankoo,
> Boggabri, narrabri, nevertie, yanchor,
> Hoopla! Hoopla! Ha-Ha-Ha!
> Yanchor High School Ya-Ya-Ya!"

Welcome to Woop Woop and the outback in Australian cinema

Imagine this: there is a cinema screen mounted on top of Uluru, as big as the rock itself, and it is playing *Welcome to Woop Woop*. It is night-time. A giant hand grips a pen that writes in light, and draws a fury of arrows from the action on the screen to the constellations in the firmament, each of which represents an Australian film of the past. As Teddy's fate is played out and he stages his escape with Krystal we start to see that the entire sky has been covered with lines and linkages because so much of the nation's film history is revisited and repurposed in Elliott's film.

Not all of it, by any means. No *The Getting of Wisdom*, or *Let the Balloon Go*, or *40,000 Horsemen*. But there are echoes, conscious or otherwise, of a whole slice of our film history, most notably the ocker-populist end of the continuum and films shot in the Australian interior. That not-so-dead heart is at the heart of our film-making history.

Give yourself five minutes to circumnavigate the nation by film. Make like a cineaste Matthew Flinders. We are one of the most urbanised nations on earth, with a population stuck limpet-like to the coast, so it makes sense that we have films beaded along the continent's littoral. A back-of-the-envelope list, starting randomly on the Coorong in South Australia with *Storm Boy*. Tasmania – *The Tale of Ruby Rose*; *The Sound of One Hand Clapping*; *Oscar and Lucinda*. Melbourne and environs offer the eponymous trifecta of *Death in Brunswick*, *Spotswood*,

Hotel Sorrento. To Eden, for the wonderful *High Tide*, and beautiful Bermagui for the less marvellous *The Man Who Sued God*. The Sutherland Shire, sparkling like Passion Pop in *Puberty Blues*. Bellingen for *Danny Deckchair*. Coolangatta for *Coolangatta Gold* and *Muriel's Wedding*. *Eliza Fraser* on Fraser Island, and *Dead Calm* on the Barrier Reef. Port Douglas for the northern destination in *Travelling North*. *Charlie and Boots* on Cape York. Up in the Top End, problematic *Yolngu Boy* and the classy *Ten Canoes*. *Crocodile Dundee* in Kakadu. Darwin for *Last Cab to Darwin*. *Bran Nue Dae* in Broome. *Japanese Story*, Port Hedland. *Under the Lighthouse Dancing* on Rottnest Island. Back to South Australia, finishing the journey in Port Lincoln with another Greg Rowe film, *Blue Fin*.

There are hinterland movies: *Romulus, My Father*. *Babe*. *The Cars That Ate Paris*. *Sirens*. *The Coca-Cola Kid*. A few high country excursions such as *The Man from Snowy River* and *The Silver Brumby*. The suburbs, a setting little used for the majority of our film history, are now of greater interest: *The FJ Holden*. *Little Fish*. *My Year Without Sex*. *Sweetie*. *Strictly Ballroom*.

And then there are the movies of the interior – and they are legion. From the earliest days of the Aussie film industry, cinema visionaries have turned their lenses towards the centre. Early examples include *Way Outback* (1911); *The Girl from Outback* (1911); *Into Australia's Unknown* (1915); and *A Romance of the Burke and Wills Expedition of 1860* (1918). The arrival of colour made the desert even more alluring for cinematographers – red dirt, golden sun, expanses of blue sky. The first local film to eschew black and white, *Jedda*, was shot on Gevacolor in central Australia.

For the remainder of the twentieth century filmmakers tried with different levels of success to capture the outback on colour film. Movies as diverse as *Walkabout, The Man from Hong Kong, Rikky and Pete, Backlash, Mad Max 2, Burke and Wills, Wills and Burke, Backroads,* and scores of others, gloried in the harsh beauty of the central

Australian landscape.

Few were shot better than *Welcome to Woop Woop*. Cinematographer Mike Molloy had been a camera operator on *Walkabout* a quarter of a century earlier but had rarely been in the outback since. Somehow he coaxed his Panavision cameras to pick up the flintiness of the desert in summer, the sunlight fracturing the landscape, the epochal triumph of minerals that endure while animals and vegetables wilt.

Despite being a Sydneysider with no special exposure to the Australian outback film canon, Elliott – in harness with Molloy and his art and design team – made a film that picked the eyes from all preceding outback movies. Perhaps Elliott was responding to the locale rather than precedent films; he had certainly spent time in the outback itself, looking and thinking and talking – and it could be that different film visionaries will see the same key features in any given environment, and conceive similar ways in which to shoot them. Or it could be the creative input from his team was strong and drew on individuals' own experiences and viewing histories. Or perhaps Elliott is a cinematic equivalent of that remarkable desert critter the thorny devil (moloch horridus) which does not drink with its mouth but rather absorbs moisture through the skin of its belly; maybe Elliott's artistic vision is a permeable membrane which can soak up ideas from everywhere before refashioning them into something original and all his own.

Relevant antecedents can be found throughout Australian screen history, although there is no suggestion that any of these films was directly influential on the *Welcome to Woop Woop* creative team. For example, in George Marlow's 1911 *Driving a Girl to Destruction*, "the wealthy hero, Robert Ray, wakens from a drinking bout to find himself married to Ruth, a 'brandy nymph', who announces later that she is pregnant."[102]

In the 1923 Beaumont Smith movie *Prehistoric Hayseeds*, "A university student…investigates claims that a prehistoric race still lives in the Australian outback. With the aid of the Hayseeds, he finds the sole surviving family of the lost tribes, the Wups, living in a cave and wearing clothes made of rabbit-skin."[103] Welcome to Wup-Wup?

The 1931 musical *Showgirl's Luck* features a song, 'The Swaggy Chorus', performed by a gaggle of women in bright matching shorts and lariats executing a knee-bending dance beneath a huge stylised wooden kangaroo, which has a brio that links to Elliott's playful vision of what our nation is or could be.

Reverberations of Daddy-O's rallying words can be found in the great speech delivered by Dad in the 1932 version of *On Our Selection* (which could be taken as an address to the whole nation as the Depression began to bite): "For years I've faced and fought the fires, the floods and the droughts of this country. I came here and I cut a hole in the bush when I hadn't enough money to buy a billy can with, or a shirt to put on me back. I worked hard and honest, living on dry bread, harrowing me bit of wheat in with the brambles…The cattle perished and died before me very eyes, but…me spirit was never broken."

Interest in the outback has fluctuated. There was a peak in the 1950s with *The Back of Beyond* made on the Birdsville track by Tasmanian John Heyer; Peter Finch in *The Shiralee; Smiley* (which had its linguistic edges burnished so as not to limit foreign sales; 'yabbies' were rebranded as 'crayfish', for example); *Dust in the Sun*; and even the 1957 version of *Robbery Under Arms* moved the action from the goldfields and New England to outback locations shot in the Flinders Ranges and Bourke.

The next surge in interest was during the period of national navel-gazing, the 1970s. A new generation of moviemakers discovered the unique challenges and rewards of trying to film central Australia. Sometimes, such as in *Raw Deal*, the outback was made into anywhere – in that film Gus Mercurio, Gerard Kennedy and gang rode seven-abreast on horseback through arid country, looking like refugees from a spaghetti western. A movie from the same period, *Long Weekend* (1978 version) took a different tack and exploited every nuance of the native environment to engender dread. *Road Games* tried something similar. *Quigley Down Under*, another film with its eye on the international market, was ably shot by David Eggby but looks more like Death Valley than the Australian outback.

Cinema screens are big. This means the potential to create hyper-intimacy when subjects are shown in close up; a face or a hand can be the size of a blue whale, stretched from one wall of the theatre to the other. In *Smiley*, for example, the audience was invited to let its gaze linger on the wonderful Australian contours of Chips Rafferty's face, a continent compressed into a countenance.

However the scale of the cinema screen also provides a canvas for Big Visual Ideas. Extraordinary set design. Panoramas that elicit gasps. Image-smithing that shares a spirit with contemporary art installation work. *Where the Green Ants Dream* is ultimately unsatisfying, but all shortcomings are obviated by the indelible sight of Mrs Strehlow (Colleen Clifford), an old woman wearing a lace collar and Barbara Cartland make-up, sitting under a parasol on a steel chair with a thermos beside a small plate of fly-blown dog food, surrounded by desert. Play that bit on a loop in the Tate Modern and no-one would complain.

The lightly-regarded *Quigley Down Under* has an epic scene where the bullies of the British army back down when confronted by hundreds of Aboriginal warriors standing in mute resistance across the horizon. It must have been hellish to stage, but it is a phenomenal image. It shares some similarities with a scene in the Maureen O'Hara vehicle *Kangaroo* where scores of Aboriginal men march in a line across the desert, wait for permission from the landholder, then drink from a seemingly endless concrete water trough.

By contrast, the predominantly suburban *Sweetie* includes a small, beautifully crafted outback scene which works through the allusive power of strangeness. Gordon (Jon Darling) drives into the desert, a sentimental country song is sung by Dorothy Barry and a cowboy dances with a chair, like a lost scene from a Hollywood musical viewed on Opposite Day. Later, two male cowhands practice their dance moves together. We see various men dancing with other men, one of whom is a dwarf.

Still, the biggest visual idea is always the landscape itself, and puny humans' place within it. Ross Gibson said that, "the majority of Australian features have been about landscape," and he is right.[104] Philip Brophy wrote that, "The taming of the land and its 'terrible beauty' is possibly the major theme which underscores all mythical narratives of Australian identity," and this is certainly true of film.[105]

Cameras pay fealty to this untameable land. The landscape has never looked more vast than in *Beneath Clouds*, where Ivan Sen and cinematographer Allan Collins placed their newcomer lead actors in exteriors of frightening size and power. Peter Weir contrived a memorable set piece in *The Last Wave*, showing the schoolhouse in the middle of red desert suppurated with heat until rain suddenly arrives – which turns rapidly to hail that smashes the glass windows and provokes wholesale horror.

In *Razorback*, DOP Dean Semmler captured painterly landscapes in brilliant oranges and reds. By contrast, *The Last of the Knucklemen*, shot around Andamooka, showed dirt that was more tawny than red, and it is only in the closing scene when Pansy and Tarzan finally start fighting that the colour starts to redden and bleed. *Love Serenade* camerawoman Mandy Walker used the salt pans (rarely shown in outback cinema, perhaps due to technical difficulties, although hauntingly effective as the site where Hugo Weaving's brutal Kev abandons his son in *Last Ride*) and a bleached palette to unusual effect. The cinematography is excellent throughout *Mad Bastards*, emphasising vastness. This peaked in the stunning scene where TJ lies down on the sun-cracked clay pan of the desert and the camera roamed wide and slow, proving how far he is from anywhere.[106]

The power of the showpiece scene in *Quigley Down Under* came from placing the warriors on an escarpment, above the soldiers. While most outback movies emphasise flatness and unfeatured space, many also draw power from the use of the vertical plane, either in the landscape (the cliff that ill-fated Midget climbs when trying to escape Woop Woop; the peak from which Mad Max looks down into the refinery compound in *Mad Max 2*) or via camera angles – the amazing elevated 360-degree pan in *Wake in Fright*. The climax of *Love Serenade* takes us beyond the ruthless flatness of the town to the (literally) fatal elevation of the grain silo. *The Tracker* made use of vertical space with local Aboriginal men sometimes appearing at high vantage points, while at other times the tracking party is on the ridges surveying the country below, reminiscent of similar shots in *Bitter Springs*. Unlike the earlier movie, *The Tracker* director Rolf de Heer had the technical capacity to underscore his special concerns by the use of some of the biggest and most dramatic zoom-out shots imaginable.

Abundant visual possibilities (and perhaps some outdated anthropological motivations) have inspired international filmmakers to tackle the Australian interior as well, creating such movies as *The Overlanders*, *The Shiralee*, *The Sundowners*, *Walkabout*, and *Where the Green Ants Dream*.

An acclaimed outback film that has not aged well is Nicolas Roeg's *Walkabout*. It still has a lot to offer visually – the thin fabric of the picnic tablecloth flapping in the desert; the children's preposterous European school uniforms contrasted with ancient rockfaces; diligent cataloguing of the natural landscape such as the whorls of wind ridges in sand, the echidnas and ants, raw rock faces, a scorpion, a mole cricket – but its ethos is very much of its time. At its worst it looks like *Blue Lagoon* in the desert, with pervy flashes of the teenage girl pulling up her knickers, crotch shots, leg shots, and sucking water through a hollow stick. It is difficult to know what to make of Roeg's decision to intercut her naked gyrations in the waterhole with shots of David Gulpilil spearing and clubbing and butchering wildlife. (Is it a reference to that nasty old Australianism, 'Old enough to bleed, old enough to butcher'?) There is a spiralling effect as the film changes gears like a B-double truckie and introduces us to a surreal cork-hatted bushie running a forced labour camp where Aboriginal people manufacture kitsch Aborigine statuary. It is an outsider's view, and illustrates the ways in which *Welcome to Woop Woop* benefitted from being an inside job.

In might be noted in passing that Americans found a link between Woop Woop and the hick town of Dogpatch in *Li'l Abner*, the 1959 Melvin Frank movie based on the comic strip of the same name. Dogpatch is a ramshackle excuse for a town, surviving on the most basic forms of farming, full of fools and knaves, with character names like Mayor Dogmeat, Earthquake McGoon, Lonesome Polecat and Appassionata von Climax. The connection is simple to make – but the crucial difference is geographical. Because of the idea's universality, it is easy to imagine an isolated rural dystopia populated with in-bred bumpkins in Russia, or in Peru, or in Greenland. A visitor trapped in the perverted internal logic of an isolated community will endure certain horrors regardless of where it is on the map. But Woop Woop is Australian, and in this movie the specific matters more than the general.

Indigenous Australia and the outback film

Tom O'Regan wrote that, "the Australian presentation of 'landscape' now feels impelled to negotiate the indigenous viewpoint and presence. It cannot be so evidently empty, primeval, Other."[107] However, for non-Indigenous Australians, the ultimate Other is not the land itself but the people who originally inhabited it.

The treatment of this Other in local films has changed over time. When wild Aboriginal men attack settlers and burn their hut in Charles Chauvel's 1935 movie *Heritage*, there is no doubt whose side the audience should be on, and no consideration given as to why the attack might be happening. Chauvel's *Uncivilised* the following year showed dozens of Aboriginal men in violent conflict with each other, including graphic scenes of men with spears lodged in their faces and necks, and one man with a spear that has passed through his body. There is an uncompromising close-up of a man called Moorpil being strangled to death by the white hero (censored in the original version) and no attempt to elicit sympathy or understanding for the slain 'natives'.

The 1950 British-Australian co-production *Bitter Springs* made some effort to reference Aboriginal dispossession, although the film's concluding scene – a glib shot of the white station owner shearing a sheep alongside a local Elder – ignored the difficult questions about ownership and racial economics hinted at in the preceding 80 minutes. Deb Verhoeven wrote that in the film's pre-production period, "a series of media scandals about the treatment of these [Indigenous] actors erupted. The producers and the government faced hefty media indignation when the Aboriginal actors arrived on location in Quorn and were found to have travelled vast distances across the state in open rail carriages. The media and the parliamentary opposition were quick to point out the apparent disparity between the claims made for Aboriginal culture in *Bitter Springs* and the actual treatment of the poorly compensated Aboriginal cast members in the course of making the film."[108]

The famed *Jedda* was the first feature to show that Indigenous characters have interior lives and emotions every bit as deep and keen as anyone else. For all of its apparent good intentions, Aboriginal characters are still referred to as "those naked monkeys", the third lead is white theatre actor Paul Reynall in black-face, and teenager Ngarla Kunoth (later Rosalie Kunoth-Monks) who played the title role was homesick and miserable during the nine-month shoot and tried unsuccessfully to run away.[109] The opening title proclaims that, "To cast this picture the producer went to the primitive Aboriginee (sic) race of Australia".

Good intentions, probably, but a chasm in understanding. This was exemplified by *Journey out of Darkness*, the only film James Trainor ever made. Released in 1967 at a time of growing political heat around Indigenous affairs, its message was progressive. It showed the different forces tugging at blacktracker Jubbal after he assists a by-the-book policeman to arrest an Arrernte man for a payback killing. Jubbal has the bone pointed at him by a kadaicha man and dies, leaving the policeman to cross the desert alone with his (never named) prisoner. The Arrernte man's knowledge of the land means the policeman has to rely on him for survival. There are interesting ideas here, but nothing can erase the horrors of casting. Jubbal is played by Ed Devereaux slathered in black make-up.[110] The Arrernte prisoner is Sri Lankan singer Kamahl. They both look completely wrong, and audiences at the time apparently thought it was wrong.[111] Was the lesson learned? Well, 25 years later, in 1992, non-Indigenous Melburnian Cameron Daddo was cast as Aboriginal outback detective Bony.

When whites take Aboriginal roles it is obvious. When white filmmakers co-opt Aboriginal culture or shovel some supernatural 'Indigenous spirituality' into their creations it is less blatant and thus more insidious. The Aboriginal man (it is always a man) with inexplicable powers crops up in a number of films. As early as 1911 in *Assigned to his Wife* the white hero's faithful Aboriginal side-kick, Yacka, dives 80 metres over a cliff into a river, an impossible feat for a 'normal' (i.e. non-Indigenous) man. In *The Phantom Stockman*, The Sundowner (Chips Rafferty) is captured by cattle duffers but uses Indigenous telepathy to call up his Aboriginal sidekick Dancer who rescues him. More recently, the dignified Aboriginal leader Burnum Burnum[112] played Oondabund in *Dark Age*, a character who has an oogady-boogady connection with the killer croc and speaks in pidgin. In *The Craic* the feckless Irish backpackers are rescued from the desert by a silent Aboriginal man who delivers them to the nearest pub. The most famous scene in *Australia* had young Nullah (Brandon Walters) use mind control to stop stampeding cattle going over a cliff.

The clunkiness of the 'black magic' conceit is exemplified in *Reckless Kelly* when Bob Maza's Aboriginal character Dan says, "It's all part of Aboriginal mythology. You know, Ned: Dreaming" – a line so dire that you hope it is satire, although it appears not to be. Elspeth Tilley argued that the mysteriously helpful Indigenous figure in Australian film is, "bestial, primitive, instinctual, mystical, and obligingly ready to lend a hand to their oppressors". She saw in this portrayal a cunning inversion of colonial history, supporting "an imagining of the white as an innocent abroad, a strategy of anti-conquest".[113]

The inversion to which Tilley refers is given a different slant by historian Manning Clark's envy for the land-connection that, as non-Indigenous, he can never have. "I am ready, and so are others, to understand the Aboriginal view that no human being can ever know heart's ease in a foreign land, because in a foreign land there live foreign ancestral spirits," Clark wrote. "We white people are condemned to live in a country where we have no ancestral spirits. The conqueror has become the eternal outsider, the eternal alien. We must either become assimilated or live the empty life of a people exiled from their spiritual strength."[114] This is a dignified and thoughtful viewpoint, yet it hints that non-Indigenous Australians would even take that deep connection to Country for ourselves if only we could.

There was plenty to critique in *We of the Never Never*, but the moment when Goggle Eye (Donald Blitner) makes clear to Jeannie Gunn that she should not have intervened when a tribal man threatened his wife presents a glimpse of the many layers of misunderstanding that continue to characterise relationships between Australia's original and settler peoples. This awkwardness and (presumably unintentional) offensiveness is stark in *The Naked Country* which tries to bring a Peckinpah sensibility to an Antipodean version of a cowboys and Indians flick, with Mornington Island people used as the 'Indians'.

One of the most interesting scenes in a recent Australian film occurs near the end of the documentary *Lasseter's Bones*. Director/narrator Luke Walker is out the back of Docker River with Traditional Owner Sandy Willie. Over the course of several days and a lot of driving he presses the local man on several issues related to Willie's Country. The viewer can see that the Elder is sick of being questioned and offended by Walker's persistence, but the English-born documentary maker is painfully slow to catch on. It is a small but remarkable moment that emphasises the immense gulf between Indigenous people living a semi-traditional lifestyle and other people in this country.

Conversely, guilt about the post-1788 history of

Indigenous ill-treatment, however valid, can lead to poor art. Mainstream Australian cinema has replaced the overt racism of earlier days with the covert racism of recent times, whereby Indigenous characters are given special treatment – quasi-magical powers, or careful backstories to explain any wrongdoing. Tom E. Lewis played the outlaw Jimmie in *The Chant of Jimmie Blacksmith*; thirty-two years later he played the outlaw Jimmy in *Red Hill*. In both films he is brutal, but in both he is given a backstory to explain his sociopathic nature. Lewis is excellent in both films, and there are good dramatic reasons for his backstory in both – but it would be interesting to have an Aboriginal criminal who was merely evil rather than 'understandably bad'. When that happens it will signal a new maturity in racial relationships. Similarly, in *Backroads*, Bill Hunter's (white) character is allowed to be crazy and criminal, but Gary Foley's (black) character has a carefully explained backstory to contextualise his wrongdoing.

The best way to address these concerns is by promoting the work of Aboriginal filmmakers. There are not five Australian films better than *Samson & Delilah*, and none with more unflinching truth or integrity. Compare the authenticity of Ivan Sen's towering *Beneath Clouds* with the regrettable missteps of *Australian Rules*. *Mad Bastards* was directed by Brendan Fletcher but made as a cooperative effort with the Pigram Brothers, and it is clearly created by people who know the world it depicts. The community of Five Rivers in the Kimberley is a sad Aboriginal version of Woop Woop. The dialogue (some of it improvised) is full of profanity, but it is delivered with great naturalness – compared to, for example, the dismal spectacle of middle-class actors trying to deliver David Caesar's attempted working-class dialogue in *Idiot Box*. We can tell what is real. *Mad Bastards* is the anti-*Sapphires*, tough-minded and non-didactic.

In terms of Aboriginal representation, *Welcome to Woop Woop* broke no new ground with its treatment of Indigenous themes and characters, and the opening titles decorated with scribble that looks like central desert iconography as drawn by Ken Done are poor. Young Lionel is shiftless and wanders around with a didgeridoo, only to reappear at the end of the film when the script requires some black hocus-pocus. Otherwise Woop Woop is a white enclave. As Daddy-O says, "Abos are pretty thin on the ground." While Elliott took a soft in ascribing special powers to the only Aboriginal character, he deserves credit for reflecting a common Australian attitude rarely depicted – disdain towards Aboriginal culture due to intellectual laziness rather than active racism. So when Teddy tries to find out what 'The Big Red' is, Angie tells him it's "weird Abo shit." Duffy says, "They're full of far-out shit like that – they're Abos." It's a great line and speaks eloquently of a particular national mindset, but most filmmakers would have shied away from it, or insisted that it had to be delivered poisonously rather than laconically. In 2015 Elliott said that the dialogue between Teddy and Duffy in front of the rock art is "absolutely appalling…If we wrote dialogue like that today we'd get shot."[115]

Dead Heart was an important but overlooked film that emerged at a similar time to *Welcome to Woop Woop*. Its marketing focused on the erotic spectacle of Aaron Pedersen and Angie Milliken writhing naked beside a waterhole in a sacred Aboriginal men's site. The trailer began with the crit 'A thoughtful, exotic sizzler' from that respected film mag Playboy, signalling where they thought the audience appeal would be. In truth, Nick Parsons crafted a subtle, intelligent representation of outback racial tensions, etching characters who are never all bad or all good. Bryan Brown gives one of his best performances as Ray Lorkin, a cop struggling to retain his integrity in trying circumstances. Through its intelligence, the movie earned the right to have Lorkin blurt, "Don't give me any of that spooky Aboriginal bullshit!" – and the line, in context, is perfect. It chimes with Duffy's sentiment. It speaks to the absence of understanding, for whatever myriad reasons, between white and black Australia. It is real.

Afterword: The cannibalism conceit

As *Welcome to Woop Woop* cannibalised and re-embodied other Aussie heat and dust movies, so I endeavoured to devour the corpus of outback cinema in order to identify key elements in Elliott's film. Or, to envisage it in Woop Woop terms, I dragged the carcasses of a hundred outback films to the processing plant, and this is the end product, presented in handy canned form.

Pet theory, pet food.

I watched a lot of Australian outback films, but no doubt missed a lot more. I did not keep a tally and I do not even recall what some were called. But it was an exercise in immersion, wonderful in the main, occasionally liminal of insanity.

What did I see?

Red dirt. Big skies that go on forever, a canopy of piercing blue that stretched from one film to the next. Close-ups of stubbled faces, sweat beading on whiskers, eyes squinting. John Meillon: great, great John Meillon; corrupt and conniving and wicked and dignified and hapless, and in every role reliably exquisite. Aborigines skulking in margins, pushed almost out of frame, just on the inside of the sprocket-holes; contributing a didgeridoo solo, or looking pathetic or noble or suffering, or calling someone 'boss'. Vehicles: shitboxes, chopped yank tanks, paddock bashers, 4WDs, Holdens, big bull-nosed semis. Kangaroos, often dead. Weird lizards and remorseless ants. The front bar: the foam of beer, the close-up of glasses being emptied, the forbearance of all-knowing bar staff. Women in faded print dresses. Rocks in suggestive shapes conveying the non-specific menace of a de Chirico shadow. Roads, often empty, always endless. No-horse towns with dusty petrol bowsers and sagging verandahs. Isolated communities operating under their own rules, like a cluster of virulent cancer cells.

Place beats plot. But the every-movie plot, for what it is worth, involved lone males tangled in webs beyond their understanding, failing to shrug free, alternatively helped or hindered by amoral locals. The persistent will to escape leads to an eventual getaway which is only ever partial, and as much is lost as is gained through what must be left behind. Stop for a beer or a last look. Drive on. Roll credits.

Character? The lead character is a bloke. Outback films love men. Australians love men. The theme song from *They're a Weird Mob* should be the theme song for the Aussie film industry: 'In This Man's Country'. In *Sunday Too Far Away* the camera roams over the face, forearms and hands of Jack Thompson in orgasmic rapture as he shears a merino, fetishizing this embodiment of the Australian myth. This is the apogee of outback film man-love rather than a representative case, but it points to the notion that men are the only worthwhile subjects for these movies. And the man in question? Neither handsome nor hideous, resourceful enough to get into the mess, not resourceful enough to escape unscathed. He brings a wider world-view to which he must cling tight as the yokels try to smack it away. He relies on no-one, although a woman or an Indigenous man usually proves a useful ally, at least fleetingly. He does not engineer social change; his goal is personal escape, not communal transformation.

What do you hear with your eyes closed in the cinema? Whispers of wind, desert emptiness, lumpen rock songs, rural accents hard enough to grind chisels on, snatches of 'rightio' and 'she'll be right', the vernacular of some decades previous. Then, usually, the infusion of a sound from elsewhere – a piece of European music, for example, or American pop – reminding us of just how far we are from wherever the film is being shown. You hear the Australian voice, grinding away. Usually. Warwick Thornton's masterpiece *Samson & Delilah* achieved soul-shredding poignancy with an almost total lack of dialogue. By contrast, *Welcome to Woop Woop* has logorrhoea.

What doesn't appear? The first thing anyone encounters in the outback is flies – millions of them – but we don't see many in outback movies (*The Tracker* and *Strangerland* are two exceptions to this rule.) The next big deal out back is the lack of water. Obviously this was a feature of *The Breaking of the Drought* and *Burke and Wills*, and pivotal to the plot in *Walkabout*, *No Worries* and *Lucky Miles*, but it is curiously underplayed in many local movies. Bushfires provide dramatic potential but are underrepresented in outback films. We see kangaroos and emus – but few snakes, few feral camels or brumbies or donkeys, few of the gigantic terrifying eagles which cruise the Centre (used as an effective motif in *Rabbit-Proof Fence*, but otherwise rarely employed.) The pub is omnipresent, but we don't often get to see churches or schools or footy ovals. If there are trees, they are gums. Where are the desert oaks? Where are the wildflowers? Where are the white bureaucrats? Where are the black bureaucrats? Where are the fleets of white Toyotas? Where is the air-con?

After cannibalising every available celluloid excursion to the interior I am convinced it would be possible to edit up The One Great Australian Outback Movie without so much as a pick-up shot added to the available footage. Splice together Meillon and Bill Hunter and Chips Rafferty; select the best of all those thousands of shots of skies and roads and spinifex; choose one bar scene to establish the main plot idea, and another bar scene to resolve it. A shot from inside the vehicle on the endless road; a different shot of a menacing semi-trailer approaching. This Aboriginal face, that gecko, this roadkill roo, that broken homestead verandah – they are all interchangeable pieces of screen furniture. You can imagine it. Or I can, easily; I've already seen it, every time I closed my eyes at night during the viewing odyssey. Ninety-five minutes. A respectable effort, a little more ambitious than some, not quite fulfilling all its stated aims. Not 10BA rubbish; not Cannes-worthy either. Three-and-a-half stars.

Or alternatively, you could just watch *Welcome to Woop Woop*.

Appendix I: Outback Tropefest

Certain motifs recur in outback movies, for good reasons. Ask a variety of tailors to make a shirt from similar bolts of cloth and many will look alike. One of the fascinations of *Welcome to Woop Woop* is that it is the Australian outback movie in excelsis, with more tropes patchworked together than any other film. (*The Adventures of Priscilla, Queen of the Desert* has a lengthy checklist of outback movie tropes also, including didgeridoo music, a dead kangaroo, an outback servo, several scenes inside front bars, excellent footage of the open road, male water wrestling, an old drive-in, and music from elsewhere – in this case Joan Carden's superb 'E strano!' while the performers trail fabric from the roof of the charging Queen of the Desert.)

Aboriginal rock art

There are rock paintings in *Satellite Boy*, and at Yutica in *Blackfellas*. There is bad rock art in *Reckless Kelly* and *Jedda* and *Until The End of the World*, and paintings made to look a little like wandjinas in *Quigley Down Under*. Teddy and Duffy encounter rock art outside Woop Woop.

Ad hoc home decoration

The wrecker's yard chic of the *Mad Max* movies. Peter Whittle making a bottle-top necklace and hat-band in *Wake in Fright*. The Glenrowan Hotel in *Reckless Kelly* which looks like something constructed on Gilligan's Island. And, of course, most of the interiors in *Welcome to Woop Woop*.

The beach

The ultimate contrast to the outback. In *Backroads*, Joe has never seen the ocean (like Angie in *Woop Woop*). That film ends with a scene of mindless shooting on the beach, like so much meaningless ejaculation. The climactic fight in *Turkey Shoot* happens by the ocean, providing a sense of release from the oppressiveness of the interior. The carefree beach is used in *Wolf Creek* as the ultimate contrast to the horrors awaiting the young travellers in the desert. In *Kiss or Kill* it is a moment of relief from the characters' outback unhappiness, while in *Tracks* the Indian Ocean is a goal and a reward.

The bull male

Sadistic Arthur Burns in *The Proposition*. Peeto who fights for no good reason in *Red Dog*. Tarzan in *The Last of the Knucklemen*. The Mayor in *The Cars That Ate Paris*. Linden, leader of the 'plastic gangsters' in *Toomelah*. And Daddy-O, of course.

Dead kangaroos

Welcome to Woop Woop calls attention to this prevalent motif with a spectacular shot reflecting the night sky in a dead roo's eye. Among many other examples, we see dead kangas in *Long Weekend* (1978 version), the insane cull in *Wake in Fright*, and the unforgettably unpleasant butchering scene in *Snowtown*. In *Running on Empty* they play Spotto for dead kangaroos on the country road. *On Our Selection* (1932 version) has a dead kangaroo down a well. In *Stone Bros.* they run over then eat a roo. *The Coca-Cola Kid* changes the formula a little, with an injured kangaroo being flown to a vet. In *Australia* a kangaroo is shot dead from the roof of a truck. There are dead roos in *Red Dog* and *Crocodile Dundee* and *Backroads*. *Walkabout* shows a dead kangaroo covered in flies, but it also includes a shot in the suburban kitchen of a handful of raw roo mince. A kangaroo with its throat ripped out is carefully examined in *In The Winter Dark*. Psychopath Mick Taylor burbles "Sorry Skippy" as he runs over a roo in *Wolf Creek 2*. In the climactic hallucination scene in *Road Games*, a kangaroo with red tail-light eyes leaps out in front of the truck – a direct link to the climactic event in *Welcome to Woop Woop*.

Didgeridoos

Philip Brophy has suggested that the didgeridoo is Aboriginal sonic drag: "At its worst, the didgeridoo is applied like black-face make-up: it is the ghostly absence of an Indigenous presence, rendered as a disembodied meme upon the imagescape of a European framing of the land."[116] There is a didgeridoo played at a ceremony as painted dancers parade in *Dark Age*. A didgeridoo player busks in *The Coca-Cola Kid*. It is a subtle soundtrack inclusion at the end of the opening credits of *Evil Angels*. A didg is played in close-up in *Where the Green Ants Dream*, at a ceremony in *Jedda*, in *Broken Hill* and *Australia*, and by Young Lionel in *Welcome to Woop Woop*.

Dog food

In *Razorback* animals are shot for pet food and processed at the sinister PetPak factory. There is a plate of dog food on the desert floor in *Where the Green Ants Dream*. Max eats a can of 'Dinki-Di' dog food in *Mad Max 2*. The pup eats dog food in *Dusty* with Bill Kerr's authentic Aussie imprecation, "Get stuck into that." The gambling scene in *Red Dog* pays homage to the two-up scene in *Wake in Fright* – except in the middle of the ring of gamblers is a dog eating dog food. In Woop Woop, it is tins of Woof Woof.

Drive-ins

Pete and Old Jagamarra live in an abandoned outback drive-in in *Satellite Boy*. Miranda Otto sits on playground equipment in the defunct, overgrown drive-in in *Love Serenade*. There is a drive-in scene in *Red Dog*, and Woop Woop's denizens attend a form of drive-in, albeit without cars. In an urban setting, the car chase does a lap of a drive-in in *Alvin Purple*, and of course *Dead-End Drive-In* was a schlocky celebration of the now-faded entertainment institution.

Farting

The chronic flatulence of Woop Woop matriarch Ginger is presaged by the persistent farting of Deadeye Dick in *The True Story of Eskimo Nell*. *Kangaroo Jack* has a camel that farts. If you removed the fart jokes from *Ned* there would be little left, and there is flatus fun in *Ten Canoes*. More urban if not urbane, Shaz lights her own farts in *Mental*.

Fascination with/Fetishisation of cars (other than Kombis)

Welcome to Woop Woop offers a 1968 Hillman Hunter and a 1953 Holden ute once the action moves to Australia, as well as the thumping huge Wabco 35C rock truck.[117] In *Running on Empty* there is a '57 Chevy Coupe, Ford Falcon GTHO Phase III XY, Dodge Challenger, HK Monaro (which gets rissoled) and what looks like a hotted-up Holden Special. In the *Mad Max* trilogy and *The Cars That Ate Paris* the vehicles are elevated to the status of central characters. In *Cactus* writer-director Jasmine Yuen Carrucan emphasises the inhospitable bush by having city-boy John drive his 1972 Ford Fairmont into the outback where the roughneck cop wears a Holden belt-buckle, the servo owner has a Holden t-shirt and every other car he sees – a Commodore ute, a one-tonner and a Rodeo – is a Holden.

Fire

In *Radiance* the redemptive fire comes when the sisters burn down the house of memories. *The*

Overlanders shows the homestead being torched before the farmers drove their cattle south, in accordance with the scorched earth policy to prevent invading Japanese using existing resources. Bushfires are pivotal in *The Breaking of the Drought* and *The Squatter's Daughter*; the latter is particularly frightening, apparently an accurate representation of the actual fire on the shoot which was fuelled with nitrate film, diesel and sump oil, and was temporarily out of control. In *Walkabout* there is a car ablaze in the desert. Mick Taylor torches a different car for a different reason in a different desert in *Wolf Creek*. The young mates set a campervan ablaze in *Satellite Boy*. In *Welcome to Woop Woop* it is the garbage pile funeral pyre.

Foreigners[118]

For reasons of box-office appeal, international sales or cultural cringe, there is a lengthy tradition of casting foreign leads in Australian films. Early examples include American Muriel Starr in *Within the Law* (1916); American Fred Niblo in *Get-Rich-Quick-Wallingford* (1916); Irishwoman Sara Allgood in *Just Peggy* (1918); American Hedda Barr in *The Man from Snowy River* (1920 version); Brits John Longden and Charlotte Francis in *The Silence of Dean Maitland* (1934); American Helen Twelvetrees in *Thoroughbred* (1936); and Englishman Dennis Hoey as the lead in Charles Chauvel's *Uncivilised* (1936). In more recent times, and more explicitly outback settings: Jamie Lee Curtis' vulnerable American hitchhiker in *Road Games*; the peripatetic pom Venneker in *The Sundowners*; Laurence Breuls and Joanne Froggatt as the unfortunate Brits in *Murder in the Outback*; Jim Cavizel in Long Weekend (2008 version); the American Carl Winters played by Gregory Harrison in *Razorback*; and our man Johnathon Schaech. Their general experience of the outback is summed up by British Captain Stanley in *The Proposition*, who says, "Australia. What fresh hell is this?"

Front bars

Which outback movies do *not* have scenes inside pubs? *The Umbrella Woman* has love interest Sam Neill working behind the bar. In *Lucky Miles* it is the first point of intersection with white Australia for the discombobulated boat people. In *Blackfellas* the bar represents backsliding. In *The Sundowners* it means good cheer. In *Wake in Fright* it is a lower circle of hell. In *Crocodile Dundee* it is the convivial place where the house entertainment is punching a patron in the guts while he balances a beer on his head. In *Razorback* it is insanely hostile. In *Mystery Road* it is where Detective Jay Swan sips iced water while his sergeant downs a morning beer. In *Backlash* it is where a very different cop screams at his female colleague. In *Nickel Queen* it is the setting for the opening scene showing the normality of local life before the arrival of dope-smoking sex maniac The Guru, played by John Laws (yes, really: *that* John Laws.) It is where Frank meets Neverest's policeman in *Swerve*. The school choir rehearses amongst the drinkers of Kookaburra Springs at the Mayfair Hotel in *Sunstruck*. In *The Picture Show Man* it is where John Meillon checks his bank roll. In *Welcome to Woop Woop* it is where the town meets at the end of each day – and on and on it goes.

The isolated town, always shot from above and from a distance

Woop Woop. The Yabba. Paris. The insular enclaves in *Mad Max 2* and *Until the End of the World*. Wala Wala in *Dead Heart*. Nathgari in *Strangerland*. Even the desert concentration camp for 'deviants' in *Turkey Shoot* is filmed in this way.

Kombis

Teddy's Kombi in *Welcome to Woop Woop* is but one of many. (It was even one of many within the movie – Elliott thinks there were six or eight used for various stages of the shoot. For the final chase scene, "We had a crane that lifted the kombi 150 feet in the air and just dropped it. It could have been a model – but it's real.") *Bran Nue Dae* has a Kombi, as does *Murder in the Outback*. *The Life of Harry Dare* is about an Aboriginal man trying to find his stolen Kombi. Dorothy's yellow Kombi crashes at the start of *Oz – A Rock n Roll Road Movie*. In *Travelling North* they travel north in a Kombi. The circus performers pull up to doctor's house in a kombi in *The Rover*. The merciful foreigners drive a Kombi in *Wolf Creek*.[119]

Music from elsewhere

Usually this means protagonists hearing non-diegetic songs, emphasising how far away they are, as in *The Cars That Ate Paris* when Arthur drives out of town to the sound of the French song 'L'ame des poetes'. In *Dimboola* the dignified brass band music counterpoints the local disposition. The booming Barry White soundtrack is splendidly out of synch with the world of *Love Serenade*. The juke box in *Backroads* plays tunes that do not belong. Faure's 'Requiem' is thrown against the landscape in *Where the Green Ants Dream*. Victoria de los Ángeles and Carlo del Monte sing Verdi gorgeously and incongruously at several points in *Incident at Raven's Gate*. The injection of Keli Hilson's 'Pretty Girl Rock' into the world of *The Rover* is suitably bizarre.

When Hiromitsu Tachibana drives his car in the Western Australian desert in *Japanese Story* he hears Yothu Yindi on the radio; in this inversion, the music is local (albeit from 4,000 kilometres away) and the listener is from elsewhere. The most bizarre occurrence is probably in *Dingo* when Miles Davis lands his jet on an outback airstrip and the locals pile out of the Poona Arms Hotel to have their minds blown by his impromptu blast of Parisian jazz fusion. In terms of the prevalence of this trope, Woop Woop's whacky R & H fascination is as much rule as exception.

Naked and semi-naked all-male showering, horseplay or wrestling in water

Featured in *Backroads, The Last of the Knucklemen, Lucky Miles, Buddies, Young Einstein* – and the city story *They're a Weird Mob*. There is a tender variation of this trope when Rex and Tilly swim in a waterhole in *Last Cab to Darwin*. Eschewed in *Welcome to Woop Woop*, although Teddy showers naked outdoors, albeit alone.

One-pump servos in two-dog towns

Blind Wally's establishment is an unforgettable feature of the road towards Woop Woop. Similarly significant are the Shell servo in *The Cars That Ate Paris* and Rebel's servo in *Running on Empty*. Additionally there is the servo with the racist attendant in *Stoned Bros.*, and the one where Bruce Spence is overcharged for his two bucks of Super in *Oz – A Rock n Roll Road Movie*, and the one operated by Julie McGregor's husband that she flees in *Backroads*, and the one run by reclusive Tom McGregor in *Back of Beyond*, and the Golden Fleece in Dungatar in *The Dressmaker*, and several different ones in *Kiss or Kill*. There is also a garage run by the victim's father in *Shame*, and a garage where Dooley works briefly in *Blackfellas*, albeit in slightly bigger country towns.

The out of place oddball, tolerated by locals

John Hurt's eye-rolling Jellon Lamb in *The Proposition*. Max Cullen's memorable Reb, the rockabilly-loving blind mechanic and demonic speed fiend from *Running on Empty* who could slot straight into Woop Woop without missing a beat. Albert the nudist, proprietor of Emperor's Palace in *Love Serenade*. David Argue's Dicko, an aggro local worker with a preference for camp attire in *Razorback*. And Reggie, Woop Woop's renegade medico.[120]

Pigs

Teddy shares a shit-sluiced pen with a pig in *Welcome to Woop Woop*. We see the old couple with a pig in a crib in *Dimboola*. Stacy Keach drives a truck loaded with pig carcasses in *Road Games*. The pigs are alive in the back of Paul Chubb's vehicle when he comes to the rescue of the lawn bowlers in the car crash that kicks off *Road to Nhill*. There is a mad pig in *Razorback*, a cute pig in *Babe*, pigs shot in *Wolf Creek*, and a wild boar charging out of the rainforest in *Crocodile Dundee 2*.

Road shots

Well, obviously. The road into the eerie otherworldly landscape in *Lake Mungo*. The dirt road in *The Sundowners* on which two truckloads of eager shearers somehow contrive to bingle. The back road which becomes malevolent in *Wrong Side of the Road* when the band is stopped by police with fascistic tendencies. The long, long zoom to a lone motorbike rider on the Broken Hill-Menindee road in *Reckless Kelly*. Etcetera.[121]

Trucks

If cars are the native fauna of Australian movies, big rigs are the prevailing introduced species. A semi causes a near-collision in *Doing Time for Patsy Cline*. A big rig tailgates the escaping duo in *Kiss or Kill* before trying to run them off the road. A vicious dust storm causes a sheep truck to overturn in *No Worries*. A B-triple rumbles through darkness in the stunning first shots of *Mystery Road*. The road train in *Cactus*, shot stylishly from bitumen level as it drives towards us, stops in the middle of the outback at a sign saying 'Road closed due to flooding', although Bryan Brown's cop on the other end of the CB avers that "We're at the arse-end of a hundred year drought." The salty-tongued driver of the truck zooming past the parked Kombi in *Welcome to Woop Woop* is director Elliott.

The vernacular

Flattened vowels, minimised consonants, mild profanity. You beaut. The use of heavy vernacular has long been part of Australian movie making, including films like *The Sentimental Bloke* (1919), *Ginger Mick* (1920) and *The Dinkum Bloke* (1923). In *Tall Timber* (1926) the titles were written by Sydney journalist Jim Donald, "and apparently attempted to achieve some degree of colloquial flavour, for the 'Sydney Morning Herald', 23 August 1926, commented that the film-makers have 'striven to give Australian atmosphere by loading [the captions] with slang, so that the effect is not only exaggerated, but at times positively displeasing.'"[122]

The vernacular gives us quintessentially Aussie lines like, "Y'r mad, ya bastard." (*Wake in Fright*); "Tell tale tittle tat!" (*Smiley*); "Workin? What would ya wanna do that for?" (*Blackfellas*); and "Ya mad bugger." (*Crocodile Dundee*). As Daphne Campbell gallops alongside the army convoy in *The Overlanders* a soldier shouts "Take a gig at the sheila!" before someone else says "You beaut" and the scene is rounded out with "Good on yer, digger". Macauley observes that "hoof[ing] it" with his daughter Buster is "Like walkin' with a flamin' mushroom" in *The Shiralee*.

There is an obscenity contest between Mexico Pete and Bogger in *Eskimo Nell*. The hideous stasis of *Toomelah* is summed up by Michael the alcoholic who says, "Every cunt always in a hurry to go nowhere." Ugly local vernacular moves from the aural to the visual with graffiti on an outback toilet wall in *Road Games*: 'don't root abos mate', and the treasonous 'slim dusty is a poofter'.[123]

Appendix II: Ask for it by name

Belgium: Bienvenue à Woop Woop
Finland: Tervetuloa Woop Woopiin
Greece: Kalos irthate sto... Pouthena!
Hungary: Woop Woop – Az isten háta mögött
Italy: Benvenuti a Woop Woop
Poland: Witajcie w krainie Woop Woop

Appendix III: Films referred to in this book

Format: Australian release title (Director, Year of release)

40,000 Horsemen (Charles Chauvel, 1941)
A Few Best Men (Stephan Elliott, 2011)
A Romance of the Burke and Wills Expedition of 1860 (Charles Byers Coates, 1918)
After Hours (Martin Scorsese, 1985)
Aguirre: The Wrath of God (Werner Herzog, 1972)
Alvin Purple (Tim Burstall, 1973)
Apocalypse Now (Francis Ford Coppola, 1979)
As Time Goes By (Barry Peak, 1988)
Assigned to His Wife (Jack Gavin, 1911)
Australia (Baz Luhrmann, 2008)
Australian Dream (Jackie McKimmie, 1987)
Australian Rules (Paul Goldman, 2002)
Babe (Chris Noonan, 1995)
Back of Beyond (Michael Robertson, 1995)
Backbeat (Iain Softley, 1994)
Backlash (Bill Bennett, 1987)
Backroads (Phillip Noyce, 1977)
Bad Boy Bubby (Rolf de Heer, 1993)
Barry McKenzie Holds His Own (Bruce Beresford, 1974)
Beneath Clouds (Ivan Sen, 2002)
Big Red (Norman Tokar, 1962)
Bitter Springs (Ralph Smart, 1950)
Blackfellas (James Ricketson, 1993)
Blue Fin (Carl Schultz/Bruce Beresford, 1978)
Bootmen (Dein Perry, 2000)

Boronia Boys (Timothy Spanos, 2009)
Boxing Day (Kriv Stenders, 2007)
Bran Nue Dae (Rachel Perkins, 2009)
Breaker Morant (Bruce Beresford, 1980)
Brigadoon (Vincente Minnelli, 1954)
Broken Hill (Dagen Merrill, 2009)
Buddies (Arch Nicholson, 1983)
Burke and Wills (Graeme Clifford, 1985)
Cactus (Jasmine Yuen Carrucan, 2008)
Charlie and Boots (Dean Murphy, 2009)
Coolangatta Gold (Igor Auzins, 1984)
Crocodile Dundee (Peter Faiman, 1986)
Crocodile Dundee 2 (John Cornell, 1988)
Cunnamulla (Dennis O'Rourke, 2000)
Dad and Dave Come to Town (Ken G. Hall, 1938)
Danny Deckchair (Jeff Balsmeyer, 2003)
Dark Age (Arch Nicholson, 1987)
Date Night (Shawn Levy, 2010)
Dead Calm (Phillip Noyce, 1989)
Dead End Drive-In (Brian Trenchard-Smith, 1986)
Dead Heart (Nick Parsons, 1996)
Death in Brunswick (John Ruane, 1990)
Deliverance (John Boorman, 1972)
Dimboola (John Duigan, 1979)
Dingo (Rolf de Heer, 1991)
Dogs in Space (Richard Lowenstein, 1986)
Doing Time for Patsy Cline (Chris Kennedy, 1997)
Don's Party (Bruce Beresford, 1976)
Driving a Girl to Destruction (George Marlow, 1911)
Dust in the Sun (Lee Robinson, 1958)
Dusty (John Richardson, 1983)
Easy Virtue (Stephan Elliott, 2008)
Evil Angels (Fred Schepisi, 1988)
Eye of the Beholder (Stephan Elliott, 1999)
Fat Pizza vs. Housos (Paul Fenech, 2014)
Finding Graceland (David Winkler, 1998)
Four Weddings and a Funeral (Mike Newell, 1994)
Frauds (Stephan Elliott, 1993)

Gallipoli (Peter Weir, 1981)
Get-Rich-Quick Wallingford (Fred Niblo, 1916)
Ginger Mick (Raymond Longford, 1920)
Head On (Ana Kokkinos, 1998)
Hearts of Darkness: A Filmmaker's Apocalypse (Fax Bahr & George Hickenlooper, 1991)
Heritage (Charles Chauvel, 1935)
High Tide (Gillian Armstrong, 1987)
Hotel Sorrento (Richard Franklin, 1995)
Idiot Box (David Caesar, 1996)
Incident at Raven's Gate (Rolf de Heer, 1988)
In The Winter Dark (James Bogle, 1998)
Into Australia's Unknown (Francis Birtles, 1915)
It's Not the Size that Counts (Ralph Thomas, 1974)
Japanese Story (Sue Brooks, 2003)
Jedda (Charles Chauvel, 1955)
Journey Out Of Darkness (James Trainor, 1967)
Just Peggy (J. A. Lipman, 1918)
Kangaroo (Lewis Milestone, 1952)
Kangaroo Jack (David McNally, 2003)
Killing Priscilla (Lizzy Gardiner, 1999)
Kiss or Kill (Bill Bennett, 1997)
Lake Mungo (Joel Anderson, 2008)
Lasseter's Bones (Luke Walker, 2013)
Last Cab to Darwin (Jeremy Sims, 2015)
Last Ride (Glendyn Ivin, 2009)
Legally Blonde (Robert Luketic, 2001)
Let the Balloon Go (Oliver Howes, 1976)
Li'l Abner (Melvin Frank, 1959)
Little Fish (Rowan Woods, 2005)
Long Weekend (Colin Eggleston, 1978)
Long Weekend (Jamie Blanks, 2008)
Love Serenade (Shirley Barrett, 1996)
Lucky Miles (Michael James Rowland, 2007)
Mad Bastards (Brendan Fletcher, 2010)
Mad Dog Morgan (Philippe Mora, 1976)
Mad Max II (George Miller, 1981)
Man of Flowers (Paul Cox, 1983)

Mental (P. J. Hogan, 2012)
Mr Pip (Andrew Adamson, 2012)
Mullet (David Caesar, 2001)
Murder in the Outback (Tony Tilse, 2007)
Muriel's Wedding (P. J. Hogan, 1994)
My Year Without Sex (Sarah Watt, 2009)
Mystery Road (Ivan Sen, 2013)
Ned (Abe Forsythe, 2003)
Ned Kelly (Tony Richardson, 1970)
Nickel Queen (John McCallum, 1971)
Not Quite Hollywood: The Wild, Untold Story of Ozploitation! (Mark Hartley, 2008)
No Worries (David Elfick, 1994)
On Our Selection (Raymond Longford, 1920)
On Our Selection (Ken G. Hall, 1932)
On The Run (Mende Brown, 1983)
Oscar and Lucinda (Gillian Armstrong, 1997)
Our Friends, the Hayseeds (Beaumont Smith, 1917)
Oz – A Rock n Roll Road Movie (Chris Lofvén, 1976)
Performance (Nicolas Roeg, 1970)
Picnic at Hanging Rock (Peter Weir, 1975)
Possum Paddock (Charles Villiers/Kate Howarde, 1921)
Prehistoric Hayseeds (Beaumont Smith, 1923)
Pterodactyl Woman from Beverly Hills (Philippe Mora, 1997)
Quigley Down Under (Simon Wincer, 1990)
Rabbit-Proof Fence (Phillip Noyce, 2002)
Radiance (Rachel Perkins, 1998)
Raw Deal (Russell Hagg, 1977)
Razorback (Russell Mulcahy, 1984)
Red Hill (Patrick Hughes, 2010)
Reckless Kelly (Yahoo Serious, 1993)
Red Dog (Kriv Stenders, 2011)
Rikky and Pete (Nadia Tass, 1988)
Road Games (Richard Franklin, 1981)
Road to Nhill (Sue Brooks, 1997)
Robbery Under Arms (Jack Lee, 1957)
Romulus, My Father (Richard Roxburgh, 2007)

Running on Empty (John Clark, 1982)
Samson and Delilah (Warwick Thornton, 2009)
Satellite Boy (Catriona McKenzie, 2012)
Saturday Night Fever (John Badham, 1977)
Shame (Steve Jodrell, 1988)
Shock Treatment (Jim Sharman, 1981)
Showgirl's Luck (Norman Dawn, 1931)
Sirens (John Duigan, 1993)
Smiley (Anthony Kimmins, 1956)
Snowtown (Justin Kurzel, 2011)
Spotswood (Mark Joffe, 1992)
Stone Bros. (Richard Frankland, 2009)
Storm Boy (Henri Safran, 1976)
Strangerland (Kim Farrant, 2015)
Strictly Ballroom (Baz Luhrmann, 1992)
Sunday Too Far Away (Ken Hannam, 1975)
Sunstruck (James Gilbert, 1972)
Sweetie (Jane Campion, 1989)
Swerve (Craig Lahiff, 2011)
Tall Timber (Dunstan Webb, 1926)
Ten Canoes (Rolf de Heer, 2006)
That Thing You Do! (Tom Hanks, 1996)
The Adventures of Priscilla, Queen of the Desert (Stephan Elliott, 1994)
The Adventures of Barry McKenzie (Bruce Beresford, 1972)
The Back of Beyond (John Heyer, 1954)
The Birds (Alfred Hitchcock, 1963)
The Blue Lagoon (Randal Kleiser, 1980)
The Breaking of the Drought (Franklyn Barrett, 1920)
The Cars That Ate Paris (Peter Weir, 1974)
The Castle (Rob Sitch, 1997)
The Chant of Jimmie Blacksmith (Fred Schepisi, 1978)
The Coca-Cola Kid (Dusan Makvejev, 1985)
The Craic (Ted Emery, 1999)
The Dinkum Bloke (Raymond Longford, 1923)
The Dressmaker (Jocelyn Moorhouse, 2015)
The FJ Holden (Michael Thornhill, 1977)

The Getting of Wisdom (Bruce Beresford, 1978)
The Girl from Outback (Australian Life Biograph Company, 1911)
The Hills Have Eyes (Wes Craven, 1977)
The Last of the Knucklemen (Tim Burstall, 1979)
The Last Wave (Peter Weir, 1977)
The Laugh On Dad (A. C. Tinsdale, 1918)
The Life of Harry Dare (Aleksi Vellis, 1995)
The Man from Hong Kong (Brian Trenchard-Smith, 1975)
The Man from Snowy River (Beaumont Smith, 1920)
The Man from Snowy River (George Miller, 1982)
The Man Who Sued God (Mark Joffe, 2001)
The Marsupials: The Howling III (Philippe Mora, 1987)
The Naked Country (Tim Burstall, 1985)
The Odd Angry Shot (Tom Jeffrey, 1979)
The Overlanders (Harry Watt, 1946)
The Phantom Stockman (Lee Robinson, 1953)
The Picture Show Man (John Power, 1977)
The Proposition (John Hillcoat, 2005)
The Rover (David Michod, 2014)
The Sapphires (Wayne Blair, 2012)
The Sentimental Bloke (Raymond Longford, 1919)
The Shiralee (Leslie Norman, 1957)
The Silence of Dean Maitland (Ken G. Hall, 1934)
The Silver Brumby (John Tatoulis, 1993)
The Sound of Music (Robert Wise, 1965)
The Sound of One Hand Clapping (Richard Flanagan, 1998)
The Squatter's Daughter (Ken G Hall, 1933)
The Sundowners (Fred Zinnemann, 1960)
The Tale of Ruby Rose (Roger Scholes, 1987)
The Time Machine (George Pal, 1960)
The Tracker (Rolf de Heer, 2002)
The Story of the Kelly Gang (Charles Tait, 1906)
The True Story of Eskimo Nell (Richard Franklin, 1975)
The Umbrella Woman (Ken Cameron, 1987)
The V.I.P.s (Anthony Asquith, 1963)
The Waybacks (Arthur W. Sterry, 1918)

The Year My Voice Broke (John Duigan, 1987)
They're a Weird Mob (Michael Powell, 1966)
Thoroughbred (Ken G. Hall, 1936)
Toomelah (Ivan Sen, 2011)
Tracks (John Curran, 2013)
Travelling North (Carl Schultz, 1987)
Turkey Shoot (Brian Trenchard-Smith, 1982)
Uncivilised (Charles Chauvel, 1936)
Under the Lighthouse Dancing (Graeme Rattigan, 1997)
Until the End of the World (Wim Wenders, 1991)
Wake in Fright (Ted Kotcheff, 1971)
Walkabout (Nicolas Roeg, 1971)
Way Outback (Alfred Rolfe, 1911)
We of the Never Never (Igor Auzins, 1982)
Weekend (Jean-Luc Godard, 1967)
Welcome to Woop Woop (Stephan Elliott, 1997)
Where the Green Ants Dream (Werner Herzog, 1984)
Wills and Burke (Bob Weis, 1985)
Within the Law (Monte Luke, 1916)
Wolf Creek (Greg Mclean, 2005)
Wolf Creek 2 (Greg Mclean, 2013)
Wrong Side of the Road (Ned Lander, 1981)
Yolngu Boy (Stephen Johnson, 2001)
Young Einstein (Yahoo Serious, 1988)

Notes

1. I would take the Paul Cox masterwork *Man of Flowers*. But I would be wrong. It tells us a lot about filmmaking, about art, about frailty and emotion and the difficult work of being human, and even a bit about Australia. It does not, however, represent Australian film.
2. Asked in 2016 for her updated thoughts on the film, Basile made this interesting observation via email: "I think the whole process of reviewing is flawed. Who the hell am I to pass judgment? Or anyone for that matter? On the other hand, if you're an artist that puts something out into the world, you have to be brave."
3. 'Rude, Crude And F&*%In' Lewd: The Making Of Welcome To Woop Woop' by Erin Free, FilmInk, 2015
4. 'American Stories: Tales of Hope and Anger' by Michael Brissenden, UQP 2012
5. InFilm Australia, 27 June 2010
6. Movie Time, Radio National, Thursday 9 February 2006
7. http://www.theguardian.com/film/2015/feb/20/welcome-to-woop-woop-rewatched-gloriously-batty-love-letter-to-australia
8. 'The Lavender Bus: How a hit movie was made and sold' by Al Clark, Currency Press, Sydney, 1999, p 147
9. 'Babes in the Bush: The Making of an Australian Image' by Kim Torney, Curtin University Books, Fremantle, 2005, p 241
10. 'The Screening Of Australia, Volume 2, Anatomy Of A National Cinema' by Susan Dermody and Elizabeth Jacka, Currency Press, Sydney, 1988, p 52
11. 'Australian National Cinema' by Tom O'Regan, Routledge, London, 1996 p 93
12. 'Australian National Cinema' by Tom O'Regan, Routledge, London, 1996, p 245
13. When was the last time you saw a mainstream film from the USA in which the actors did not have perfect teeth? Looking at Hollywood youngsters, sculpted by gym sessions

and cosmetic surgeons and stylists until they conform as close as possible to some imagined physical ideal, is as interesting as looking at kitchen canisters. There is no joy in watching them move their cookie-cutter bodies, or bend their identikit faces into a prescribed 'range' of expressions. They are as sexy as silicon. Curiously, they are also contributing to their own obsolescence. As actors become increasingly interchangeable, as they function more like Balinese shadow-puppets than flesh that bleeds and breathes, they open the way for a future where filmmakers may prefer to work with computer-generated simulacra – more tractable, less expensive and equally expressive.

14. 'The Communist Manifesto: A Modern Edition by Karl Marx & Friedrich Engels', Verso edition, 2012, p 48
15. 'Beyond Priscilla', Wisconsin Gazette, 14 January 2010
16. 'Film Criticism as Cultural Fantasy: The Perpetual French Discovery of Australian Cinema' by Andrew McGregor, Peter Lang, 2010, p 257
17. 'Trajectories realign', The Australian, 7 March 2009
18. https://www.parliament.nsw.gov.au/prod/parlment/hansart.nsf/V3Key/LC20151015020
Text reproduced exactly as it appears in Hansard. This was not Dr Phelps' most remarkable parliamentary moment: that came in March 2016 when he made reference to anal fisting in a debate on the legality of eyeball tattooing.
19. This idea and wording draws from my essay Local Lunar Landings in 'Meanjin' No. 3, 2009 http://meanjin.com.au/editions/volume-68-number-3-2009/article/local-lunar-landings/
20. 'The Communist Manifesto: A Modern Edition' by Karl Marx & Friedrich Engels, Verso edition, 2012, p 40
21. I grew up in a small town. I know some great people who live in small towns. I know there can be a lot of warmth and community feeling and caring for others in small towns. But they can also be insular, repressive, reductive, depressing.
22. Quoted in 'The Bogan Delusion' by David Nichols, Affirm Press, Melbourne, 2011 , p 78
23. Smalltown (album: Songs for Drella) 1990
24. Play it all night long (album: Bad Luck Streak in Dancing School) 1980
25. 'Rude, Crude And F&*%In' Lewd: The Making Of Welcome To Woop Woop' by Erin Free, FilmInk, 2015

26. *Australian Rules* is melodramatic, clunky, lacks nuance and fails to encompass the complicated ways humans interact along and across racial lines. I call it 'ethically dubious' because of the controversy over its genesis, with local Indigenous people clearly stating they did not want the film made or screened. I spent a lot of time with a certain Kaurna Elder, a highly respected woman who held numerous honours in both white and black worlds, and the only time I ever heard her get angry or swear was in regards to this film – an indication of how deeply it hurt certain people. Given this, the film's inclusion in secondary school curriculum is bewildering. For a balanced account of the controversy, see 'Australian Rules' by Peter Ellingsen, The Age, 12 August 2002.
27. 'Australian Film 1900-1977' by Andrew Pike and Ross Cooper, OUP, 1980, p 98
28. William D. Routt, Chapter 3 of 'The Cinema of Australia and New Zealand', edited by Geoff Mayer and Ken Beattie, Wallflower Press, 2007, p 33
29. There is an interesting city counterpoint to these small-town films in the suburban grotesques of no-fi director Timothy Spanos, such as *Boronia Boys*. Spanos certainly understands how underclass Australians look, dress and what preoccupies them. He engineers dialogue that, however awkwardly delivered, nonetheless canvasses territory that is right for his characters – food courts, sausage sandwiches, fat legs in holiday photos, sexual preferences of Greek women, hangover cures. But does Spanos have contempt for his characters, putting them in dogshit-ugly interiors and speaking elliptically about nothings, or is he documenting a group that is routinely ignored? Spanos' stance towards his subjects is a lot more opaque than, for example, Paul Fenech in his cynical and highly profitable *Fat Pizza vs. Housos*.
30. *Video Killed the Radio Star*, directed by Scott Millaney, Sparkvale/Master Entertainment 2013
31. 'Rude, Crude And F&*%In' Lewd: The Making Of Welcome To Woop Woop' by Erin Free, FilmInk, 2015
32. Adrian Martin, Nurturing the Next Wave: What is Cinema? in 'Back of Beyond: Discovering Australian Film and Television', Ed. Scott Murray, AFC, Sydney, 1988, p 97
33. As it happens, it is also where Leigh Bowery grew up – an artist whose influence and international standing will last when *The Castle* is long forgotten. My tribute:

www.michaelwinkler.com.au/PDF/Leigh%20Bowery.pdf
34. 'Australian Cinema After Mabo' by Felicity Collins and Therese Davis, Cambridge University Press, 2005, p 161
35. http://encore.com.au/red-dog-red-collar-worker-9775/
36. http://www.imdb.com/title/tt0076542/trivia?ref_=tt_trv_trv
37. http://www.urbancinefile.com.au/home/view.asp?Article_ID=1419
38. Sunday Tasmanian, 16 August 1998
39. *Rod Taylor: Pulling No Punches*, directed by Robert de Young, 2016
40. The only actual footballer glimpsed in the film is a momentary shot of Justin Madden playing for Collingwood's arch-rivals Carlton on the TV screen in the founding fathers' private room. Madden went on to become a Victorian government minister. It seems doubtful that these facts are linked.
41. http://www.sbs.com.au/films/movie/1268/welcome-to-woop-woop
42. Sunday Tasmanian, 16 August 1998
43. At other times Elliott has said that the VHS cover he spotted in the Bondi video store was *The Time Machine*.
44. A skilled artist, Taylor designed the Harbord Beach Surf Club's logo
45. *Rod Taylor: Pulling No Punches*, directed by Robert de Young, 2016
46. http://www.rodtaylorsite.com/bodybeautiful.shtml
47. *Rod Taylor: Pulling No Punches*, directed by Robert de Young, 2016
48. Director commentary, 2015 release of BluRay
49. Original Production Notes, provided by Finola Dwyer
50. Production Notes
51. http://www.urbancinefile.com.au/home/view.asp?a=1432&s=features
52. http://www.urbancinefile.com.au/home/view.asp?a=1432&s=features
53. http://www.urbancinefile.com.au/home/view.asp?a=1432&s=features
54. Production Notes
55. Barnard agreed to co-produce despite Elliott claiming that he chained himself to her office door because she would not employ him on *Mad Max Beyond Thunderdome*.

56. 'Kangaroo Jack', The Chaser, 10 January 2003, p 16
57. 'Woop Woop, pedale dans le desert', Liberation, 15 May 1997; translation Melissa McMahon
58. 'Welcome to Woop Woop', Positif, no. 437-438, July-August 1997, p.111; quoted in 'Film Criticism as Cultural Fantasy: The Perpetual French Discovery of Australian Cinema' by Andrew McGregor, Peter Lang, 2010, p 258
59. 'Rude, Crude And F&*%In' Lewd: The Making Of Welcome To Woop Woop' by Erin Free, FilmInk, 2015
60. The Age, 13 August 1998
61. http://www.urbancinefile.com.au/home/view.asp?a=1432&s=features
62. The Advocate: The national gay & lesbian newsmagazine, No. 755
63. http://sensesofcinema.com/2000/feature-articles/bestandworst/
64. Last part of quote from 'Rude, Crude And F&*%In' Lewd: The Making Of Welcome To Woop Woop' by Erin Free, FilmInk, 2015
65. Sunday Herald Sun, 16 August 1998
66. New York Times, November 13, 1998
67. Entertainment Weekly, 20 November 1998
68. San Francisco Chronicle, Friday, November 13, 1998
69. Box Office, 13 November 1998
70. http://www.imdb.com/title/tt0120491/reviews?ref_=tt_ql_op_3
71. www.convictcreations.com/culture/movies/welcomewoopwoop.html
72. Possibly Pauline Hanson's lieutenant David Oldfield, who attended the Brisbane premiere in August 1998
73. http://www.sbs.com.au/films/movie/1268/welcome-to-woop-woop
74. The Sunday Age, 16 August 1998
75. Adrian Martin, The Age, 13 August 1998
76. Variety, 1 June 1997
77. 'The wise man builds his house upon the rock...the foolish man builds his house upon the sand'
78. Production Notes
79. Billboard (US edition), 28 February 1998, p 36
80. 'The Dead Heart' by Douglas Kennedy, first published 1994, Abacus edition 2012, p 37
81. The Guardian, 6 October 2006

82. 'The weight of expectations for Lloyd Jones', Sunday Age, 2 November 2013
83. 'Cinema' by Alain Badiou, Polity, Cambridge, English edition 2013
84. Playboy, 1 March 1987
85. Playboy, 1 March 1987
86. 'Intermission: A True Tale' by Anne Baxter, W. H. Allen, 1977
87. 'Tell 'Em Nothing, Take 'Em Nowhere' by Max Cullen, Pan McMillan 2010, p 188-189
88. Production Notes
89. 'Stephan Elliott is back, for better or for worse', The Australian, 21 January 2012
90. http://thehollywoodinterview.blogspot.com.au/2009/05/stephan-elliott-hollywood-interview.html
91. http://thehollywoodinterview.blogspot.com.au/2009/05/stephan-elliott-hollywood-interview.html
92. 'Stephan Elliott is back, for better or for worse', The Australian, 21 January 2012
93. 'The Lavender Bus: How a hit movie was made and sold' by Al Clark, Currency Press, Sydney, 1999, p 7
94. 'Australian National Cinema' by Tom O'Regan, Routledge, London 1996, p 156
95. 'Australian National Cinema' by Tom O'Regan, Routledge, London 1996, p 141
96. 'the adventures of priscilla, queen of the desert' by Philip Brophy, Currency Press & Australian Film Commission, 2008. Part of the Australian Screen Classics series, p 60
97. 'the adventures of priscilla, queen of the desert' by Philip Brophy, Currency Press & Australian Film Commission, 2008. Part of the Australian Screen Classics series, p 62
98. 'the adventures of priscilla, queen of the desert' by Philip Brophy, Currency Press & Australian Film Commission, 2008. Part of the Australian Screen Classics series, p7
99. 'The Lavender Bus: How a hit movie was made and sold' by Al Clark, Currency Press, Sydney, 1999, p 6-7
100. '100 Greatest Films of Australian Cinema', Ed. Scott Hocking, Scribal Publishing, Richmond, 2006, p 30
101. Scott Hocking in '100 Greatest Films of Australian Cinema', Ed. Scott Hocking, Scribal Publishing, Richmond, 2006, p 66
102. 'Australian Film 1900-1977' by Andrew Pike and Ross

Cooper, OUP, 1980, p 28
103. 'Australian Film 1900-1977' by Andrew Pike and Ross Cooper, OUP, 1980, p 119
104. Formative Landscapes in 'Back of Beyond: Discovering Australian Film and Television', Ed. Scott Murray, AFC, Sydney, 1988, p 63
105. 'the adventures of priscilla, queen of the desert' by Philip Brophy, Currency Press & Australian Film Commission, 2008. Part of the Australian Screen Classics series, p 49. Note 'terrible beauty' is a term used by Marcus Clarke in 'For The Term of His Natural Life', 1874
106. Or more correctly, how far he is from anywhere recognisable as 'safe' by a general audience. I acknowledge the point of my good friend Sam Osborne that characterising the outback as 'the middle of nowhere' marginalises those people for whom it is home.
107. 'Australian National Cinema' by Tom O'Regan, Routledge, London, 1996, p 210
108. http://sensesofcinema.com/2007/cteq/bitter-springs/
109. Elders with Andrew Denton, ABC TV, 14 December 2009
110. This was not necessarily an isolated case; in the previous year ABC-TV screened a seven-episode series, *Wandjina!*, starring white actor Julianna Allan in heavy black make-up as Aboriginal girl Linda.
111. http://www.creativespirits.info/resources/movies/journey-out-of-darkness
112. Billed as Burnham Burnham
113. 'White Vanishing: Rethinking Australia's Lost-In-the-Bush Myth' by Elspeth Tilley, Rodopi, 2012, p 94
114. 'Speaking out of Turn: Lectures and Speeches 1940-1991' by Manning Clark, Melbourne University Press, 1997, p 144
115. Director commentary, 2015 release of BluRay
116. 'the adventures of priscilla, queen of the desert' by Philip Brophy, Currency Press & Australian Film Commission, 2008. Part of the Australian Screen Classics series, p 44
117. This site is remarkable: http://www.imcdb.org/movie.php?id=120491
118. A further sub-category: Foreigners dragged in to play Aussie icons in movies with rural settings. Mick Jagger in *Ned Kelly*, Dennis Hopper in *Mad Dog Morgan*, Kirk Douglas in *The Man from Snowy River* – and, in a very different way, Meryl Streep in *Evil Angels*. A sub-category to this sub-category is

Foreigners playing Aussie archetypes: Robert Mitchum and Deborah Kerr are Aussies in *The Sundowners*. Mitchum does remarkably well, but Kerr slaughters the local accent and sounds like a wombat scratching its claws down a 44-gallon drum.

119. You can spot them in plenty of urban films too, such as *The FJ Holden*, *The Craic*, and *The Last Wave*. Anyone who has switched a 1600cc engine from a 1968 model to a 1967 split-screen knows these vehicles are comic and tragic in equal parts.

120. It is a trope in non-outback Aussie movies as well. John Hargreaves' eccentric Bung in *The Odd Angry Shot* has a function and habitude similar to Richard Moir's Reggie in *Welcome to Woop Woop*. As it happens, the admirable Moir was also in that Vietnam War movie.

121. See also artist Shaun Gladwell's gorgeous 'Approach to Mundi Mundi' (2007), a love poem to the beauty of the inland desert. He notes that he was influenced by growing up watching movies like *Razorback*, *Mad Max* and *Mad Max 2*.

122. 'Australian Film 1900-1977' by Andrew Pike and Ross Cooper, OUP, 1980, p 134

123. It is not only outback movies that revel in local language – it is a feature of many Aussie productions. The opening lines of *Dogs in Space* locate the film here and nowhere else: "Ay you, prickface. Are you from the planet Poofter or the planet Stupider?" In similar vein, the first piece of deathless dialogue in *Dead-End Drive-In* could only be Australian: "Hey fuckarse, wanna sell ya shoes?"

Acknowledgements

Many thanks to members of the cast and crew who were generous with their time and memories, most notably Stephan Elliott – an interviewer's dream.

Thanks also to Karen Ferguson, Kateal Hedley, Dov Kornits, Nadiya Luthra, Melissa McMahon, Craig Platt, Matt Price, Joe Winkler, Tim Winkler, Zac Winkler.

Sock it to me!

www.ingramcontent.com/pod-product-compliance
Lightning Source LLC
Chambersburg PA
CBHW020617300426
44113CB00007B/677